OpenStack Cookbook

Manage Compute, Storage and Networking through Single Interface

Jorven Halquin

Copyright © 2024 by GitforGits

Published by: GitforGits

Publisher: Sonal Dhandre

www.gitforgits.com

support@gitforgits.com

Printed in India

First Printing: August 2024

ISBN: 978-81-19177-80-6

Cover Design by: Kitten Publishing

For permission to use material from this book, please contact GitforGits at support@gitforgits.com.

Prologue

You are here: OpenStack Cookbook. Hello, I'm Jorven Halquin, and I've been an expert in cloud infrastructures, particularly OpenStack, for many years. I wrote this book to assist you, network administrators, engineers, and cloud specialists, in making your work with OpenStack more efficient. My goal is to share my knowledge and insights through a series of well-crafted recipes so you can have the most seamless and effective OpenStack experience possible.

Throughout this book, we will be working with an imaginary but relatable tech company called GitforGits. Initially, GitforGits operated as a small on-premise server-based software development company. Their needs for infrastructure expanded along with their business. To handle their growing number of projects and clients, they discovered that they needed better storage options, more processing power, and a more adaptable networking configuration. They decided to switch to OpenStack at that point. GitforGits selected OpenStack because of its open-source architecture and the complete control it provides over their cloud environment. But they quickly discovered, as many other organizations have, that OpenStack management can be daunting without the proper resources and expertise. This book fills that need. We meticulously crafted every recipe and chapter in this cookbook. We'll go over their issues and investigate how OpenStack can help, whether it's using Keystone for identity management, Nova for virtual machine deployment, or Neutron for complex networking configuration.

I aimed to make practicality a central theme in this book. I didn't want to limit my advice to abstract ideas or theoretical knowledge. Instead, we organize the content based on real-world issues and their corresponding solutions. We considered using OpenStack's Load Balancer as a Service, Octavia, when GitforGits needed to guarantee that their applications would always be accessible and responsive. We looked into Cinder to handle their block storage needs when they needed safe and effective storage solutions. And Heat became our go-to tool when they wanted automation to handle resource scaling because it allowed us to define infrastructure as code, guaranteeing repeatable and consistent deployments.

This book aims to empower you to take advantage of OpenStack's full potential in your own environments, not just teach you how to use it. The recipes here are as versatile as the platform itself; both are meant to be easily adjusted to suit your needs. You can use them directly in your scenarios or modify them to suit your specific requirements. I've also included troubleshooting techniques to assist you in overcoming the unavoidable hiccups on the road. I derived these solutions from my own experiences and lessons learned, addressing issues like resource allocation optimization and stack creation failures.

I hope you'll see the tremendous value that OpenStack can add to your infrastructure as we go through each chapter. Although the GitforGits story is fictional, the problems they encounter and the fixes we provide are very real. By the time this book ends, I want you to feel comfortable taking care of your OpenStack environment and have the know-how to handle any challenge that comes your way.

Content

Preface

OpenStack Cookbook is specifically tailored for cloud professionals, network administrators, and engineers who express a desire to augment their proficiency in effectively managing OpenStack environments. The book provides a pragmatic and interactive methodology with recipes that specifically target solutions to tackle the actual difficulties encountered in implementing and overseeing cloud infrastructure. Every chapter presents systematic solutions, enabling you to develop proficiency in designated OpenStack components.

These recipes provide instructions on how to install, configure, and optimize OpenStack services such as Keystone for identity management, Glance for image processing, Neutron for networking, Nova for computing management, Cinder for block storage, and Octavia for load balancing. Some of the more advanced topics covered in the book include how to use Heat for Infrastructure as Code (IaC), how to automate and repeat infrastructure deployments, and how to use Heat and Ceilometer to create auto-scaling solutions that dynamically adjust resources according to demand. Typical problems with stack creation, resource management, and orchestration tasks will be explained and solved. The book encompasses a broad spectrum of situations, ranging from the prevention of stack creation failures and template validation errors to the effective management of resource dependencies and performance issues.

With the knowledge you gain from this book, you will be able to set up, administer, and fix OpenStack environments with ease. No matter your level of expertise with OpenStack, this cookbook will equip you with the practical knowledge and solutions you need to use OpenStack efficiently in real-world scenarios.

In this book you will learn how to:

- Get the environment quickly settled with all the OpenStack services, including Nova, Keystone, Glance, and Neutron.

- Make easy management of OpenStack cloud environments a reality with these real-world solutions.

- Get your cloud infrastructure up and running consistently and reliably every time with the help of Heat templates.

- Improve your resource allocation skills with practical experience in auto-scaling with Heat and Ceilometer.

- Keep operations stable by troubleshooting common OpenStack issues and providing step-by-step solutions.

- Vertigo, XLAN, and security group configurations are just a few of the advanced networking techniques you can learn about in Neutron.

- Secure your cloud with SSL termination and volume encryption.

- Optimize traffic management and guarantee high availability by deploying Octavia-based load balancing solutions.

- Build automated cloud environment management with Infrastructure as Code (IaC).

- Get to the heart of practical problems by following recipes developed specifically for the demands of enterprise cloud infrastructure.

GitforGits

Prerequisites

This book is designed for OpenStack users, cloud professionals, networking professionals, network administrators, and cloud engineers who have solid Linux command-line skills along with basic networking knowledge. Prior knowledge of OpenStack CLI would be preferred although not mandatory.

Codes Usage

Are you in need of some helpful code examples to assist you in your programming and documentation? Look no further! Our book offers a wealth of supplemental material, including code examples and exercises.

Not only is this book here to aid you in getting your job done, but you have our permission to use the example code in your programs and documentation. However, please note that if you are reproducing a significant portion of the code, we do require you to contact us for permission.

But don't worry, using several chunks of code from this book in your program or answering a question by citing our book and quoting example code does not require permission. But if you do choose to give credit, an attribution typically includes the title, author, publisher, and ISBN. For example, "OpenStack Cookbook by Jorven Halquin".

If you are unsure whether your intended use of the code examples falls under fair use or the permissions outlined above, please do not hesitate to reach out to us at support@gitforgits.com.

We are happy to assist and clarify any concerns.

Acknowledgement

I owe a tremendous debt of gratitude to GitforGits, for their unflagging enthusiasm and wise counsel throughout the entire process of writing this book. Their knowledge and careful editing helped make sure the piece was useful for people of all reading levels and comprehension skills. In addition, I'd like to thank everyone involved in the publishing process for their efforts in making this book a reality. Their efforts, from copyediting to advertising, made the project what it is today.

Finally, I'd like to express my gratitude to everyone who has shown me unconditional love and encouragement throughout my life. Their support was crucial to the completion of this book. I appreciate your help with this endeavour and your continued interest in my career.

CHAPTER 1: SETTING UP OPENSTACK INFRASTRUCTURE

Introduction

OpenStack is a robust cloud platform, but its successful implementation starts with a well-prepared environment. This chapter will cover the critical initial steps, from preparing your hardware and configuring the operating system to installing and setting up the key OpenStack services. By the end of this chapter, you will have a fully functional OpenStack environment ready to manage and scale your cloud resources.

We will begin by addressing the hardware requirements necessary for deploying OpenStack. This involves selecting appropriate hardware, ensuring compatibility, and preparing the physical infrastructure to support a scalable and resilient cloud environment. Following this, we will run you through the process of setting up Ubuntu, the recommended operating system for OpenStack. Once the environment is prepared, we will dive into the installation and configuration of the core OpenStack services, such as Keystone for identity management, Glance for image management, Neutron for networking, Nova for compute resources, and Cinder for block storage. Each of these services plays a critical role in the functionality of your cloud, and this chapter will provide step-by-step instructions to get them up and running effectively.

Finally, we will explore how to define and implement a network topology tailored to your specific needs. This will include configuring the network components that ensure communication between different OpenStack services and your cloud infrastructure. By the end of this chapter, you will have a robust OpenStack environment, capable of supporting advanced cloud operations, ready for further customization and use in real-world scenarios.

Recipe 1: Preparing Hardware for OpenStack Deployment

Background

GitforGits, a fast-growing technology company, has reached a point where their traditional infrastructure is struggling to keep up with the demands of their expanding operations. To maintain agility and support their growth, they've decided to transition to a private cloud solution. After careful consideration, they chose OpenStack for its open-source flexibility and robust feature set. Their goal is to deploy OpenStack on their existing fleet of Linux servers, allowing them to manage compute, storage, and networking resources more efficiently. By integrating OpenStack, GitforGits aims to automate their infrastructure management, scale resources dynamically based on workload demands, and enhance overall system reliability. This book uses GitforGits as a real-world example, walking through each step of their OpenStack deployment, from initial setup to advanced configurations, offering practical solutions to the challenges they encounter along the way.

However, to ensure a successful OpenStack deployment, we need to carefully prepare the hardware on which OpenStack will run. The following steps outline how to prepare your existing Linux hardware to serve as a reliable foundation for your OpenStack cloud.

Hardware Requirements

First, assess the hardware requirements for your OpenStack deployment as the OpenStack typically requires at least two servers: one for the controller node and one or more for the compute nodes. However, in smaller environments or for testing purposes, a single node deployment may be used.

Following are the recommended hardware specifications for each node:

Controller Node

- CPU: Minimum 4 cores
- RAM: Minimum 8 GB
- Storage: Minimum 100 GB
- Network: 1 NIC for management, 1 NIC for external access

Compute Node

- CPU: Minimum 4 cores
- RAM: Minimum 16 GB
- Storage: Minimum 100 GB
- Network: 1 NIC for management, 1 NIC for external access

If you want your cloud infrastructure to grow with your business, you'll need to make sure your hardware can handle it.

Network Configuration

Here, ensure that you have at least two network interfaces on each server: one for management and one for external access. In more complex setups, additional network interfaces may be required for storage and other functions. Next, adjust the settings on each node's network interface to guarantee correct connectivity and assign IP addresses in accordance with your intended network architecture.

For GitforGits, it's important to design a network that can handle the anticipated traffic and provide redundancy where needed. So you can continue to consider using VLANs or VXLANs to segregate network traffic for management, storage, and external access.

BIOS and Firmware Configuration

Before installing the operating system, access the BIOS or UEFI firmware on each server to configure key settings for optimal performance. And then enable virtualization support (Intel VT-x or AMD-V) to allow the compute nodes to run virtual machines efficiently. Also additionally, configure the boot order to prioritize booting from the appropriate drive and disable unnecessary hardware components, such as serial ports, to streamline the system's operations.

Operating System Installation

With the hardware and network configured, now the next step is to install Ubuntu on each node as below:

- Install Ubuntu 24.04 LTS, as it provides long-term support and is compatible with the latest OpenStack releases.

- During installation, create partitions that separate the OS, OpenStack services, and data storage. This separation helps in managing storage more efficiently and allows for easier scaling.

Once the OS installation is complete, ensure that all nodes are updated to the latest security patches and that SSH access is properly configured for remote management.

Post-Installation Configuration

After installing the Ubuntu, perform the following post-installation tasks:

- Set a unique hostname for each node to easily identify them in your network.

- Configure NTP or chrony on all nodes to ensure consistent time across the network.

- Update all installed packages to the latest versions to ensure compatibility with OpenStack.

- Adjust firewall settings to allow communication between nodes on required ports, while ensuring that unnecessary ports are closed for security.

By following these steps, we (GitorGits) will have a solid hardware foundation prepared for deploying OpenStack, ensuring a smooth and scalable cloud infrastructure setup.

Recipe 2: Setting up Ubuntu for OpenStack Installation

The latest release, Bobcat (October 2023), continues to push the envelope with improved performance, security, and integrations, making it even more suitable for modern cloud environments. Bobcat enhances support for containerized workloads, offers better edge computing capabilities, and refines its core services for greater efficiency and reliability.

For GitforGits, deploying the Bobcat release of OpenStack provides the company with the latest advancements, ensuring a robust and future-proof private cloud infrastructure. In this recipe, we will install and configure the OpenStack Bobcat release on Ubuntu, thereby setting the stage for a scalable and secure cloud environment.

Preparing Ubuntu Environment

Ensure your Ubuntu system is fully updated to guarantee compatibility with OpenStack Bobcat:

```
sudo apt update

sudo apt upgrade -y

sudo apt dist-upgrade -y

sudo reboot
```

After rebooting, disable swap, as OpenStack services require it to be off for optimal performance:

```
sudo swapoff -a

sudo sed -i '/ swap / s/^/#/' /etc/fstab
```

Installing OpenStack Client

The OpenStack client is essential for managing OpenStack services via the command line:

```
sudo apt install -y python3-openstackclient
```

This client will be used throughout the setup to configure and manage services in the Bobcat release.

Adding OpenStack Bobcat Repository

First, add the repository for the OpenStack Bobcat release:

```
sudo add-apt-repository cloud-archive:bobcat

sudo apt update
```

This step ensures that you install the latest version of OpenStack services directly from the Bobcat release.

Installing OpenStack Packages

Now, install the necessary OpenStack Bobcat packages, focusing on the controller node components:

```
sudo apt install -y keystone glance nova-api nova-
conductor nova-consoleauth nova-novncproxy nova-scheduler
neutron-server neutron-plugin-ml2 neutron-linuxbridge-
agent cinder-api cinder-scheduler
```

These packages include the core services for identity, image management, compute, networking, and block storage.

Configuring Database and Messaging Services

OpenStack relies on a database and messaging service and for this, we will install and configure MySQL (MariaDB) and RabbitMQ:

- MySQL Installation

```
sudo apt install -y mariadb-server python3-pymysql

sudo mysql_secure_installation
```

- RabbitMQ Installation

Set a strong password for **root** and remove any unnecessary users.

```
sudo apt install -y rabbitmq-server

sudo rabbitmqctl add_user openstack StrongPassword

sudo rabbitmqctl set_permissions openstack ".*" ".*" ".*"
```

In the above code, replace **StrongPassword** with a secure password.

Configuring OpenStack Services

Next, configure each OpenStack service to connect to the database and messaging service. For example, in the **keystone.conf** file:

```
[database]

connection =
mysql+pymysql://keystone:StrongPassword@controller/keysto
ne


[oslo_messaging_rabbit]

rabbit_host = controller

rabbit_userid = openstack

rabbit_password = StrongPassword
```

Repeat similar configurations for all other services.

Starting the Services

After configuring, start the services and ensure they start automatically on boot:

```
sudo systemctl restart keystone

sudo systemctl enable keystone


# Repeat for all other services
```

Then, verify the installation by issuing a command to check if Keystone is functioning:

```
openstack token issue
```

This above command should return a valid token if Keystone is correctly configured and running.

With these above outlined steps, GitforGits will have the Bobcat release of OpenStack installed on Ubuntu, ensuring that the cloud environment is up-to-date with the latest features and optimizations.

Recipe 3: Installing and Configuring Keystone

OpenStack Components Overview

OpenStack is designed to control large pools of compute, storage, and networking resources, all managed through a dashboard (Horizon), command-line tools, or through an API. OpenStack allows you to deploy only the components that you need for your specific use case.

Here's a brief overview of the core 10 OpenStack components:

1. **Keystone (Identity Service)**: Manages authentication and authorization for OpenStack services. It provides a central directory of users mapped to the OpenStack services they can access.

2. **Glance (Image Service)**: Handles the discovery, registration, and retrieval of virtual machine images. It allows users to create and manage images that can be used to deploy instances.

3. **Nova (Compute Service)**: Manages the lifecycle of compute instances in an OpenStack environment. Nova orchestrates everything from launching an instance, managing its resources, to shutting it down.

4. **Neutron (Network Service)**: Provides networking as a service between interface devices managed by other OpenStack services, typically compute nodes. Neutron manages networks, subnets, routers, and provides advanced features like load balancing and firewalls.

5. **Cinder (Block Storage Service)**: Provides persistent block storage to run instances. Cinder allows you to create and manage block storage volumes that can be attached to instances for data storage.

6. **Swift (Object Storage Service)**: Stores and retrieves unstructured data objects via a RESTful, HTTP-based API. It is highly scalable and designed to store a large amount of data with redundancy.

7. **Horizon (Dashboard)**: Provides a web-based user interface to interact with OpenStack services. It allows users to manage their cloud infrastructure graphically.

8. **Heat (Orchestration)**: Automates the deployment of infrastructure, services, and applications within OpenStack through templates.

9. **Ceilometer (Telemetry)**: Collects and monitors usage data for billing, benchmarking, scalability, and statistical purposes.

10. **Trove (Database as a Service)**: Provides database management as a service, offering

deployment, management, and scaling of databases.

Introduction to Keystone

Keystone is OpenStack's identity management system and it acts as a central directory for all OpenStack services and their users, handling authentication (who can access the services), authorization (what they can do), and service discovery (which services are available). The Keystone allows users to authenticate through various methods, including username and password, token-based authentication, and external authentication systems like LDAP. By integrating with Keystone, each OpenStack service can enforce policies and access control, ensuring that only authorized users can perform specific actions.

Following are the key features of Keystone:

- Keystone can manage multiple tenants (projects) and domains, allowing for isolated environments within the same cloud infrastructure.

- Users can be assigned roles that define what actions they can perform on specific resources within a project.

- Keystone issues and manages tokens that are used by users and services to authenticate and interact with OpenStack APIs.

- Keystone provides a catalog of all available OpenStack services, their endpoints, and regions.

In order to establish a safe and controllable OpenStack environment, GitforGits must first install Keystone. To guarantee that no unauthorized users are able to access or modify cloud resources, Keystone will act as the authentication backbone. So, let's move on to installing and configuring it on the Ubuntu system running the OpenStack Bobcat release.

Install Keystone Packages

Keystone can be installed using the OpenStack package repository that was added during the previous recipe. Begin by installing the necessary Keystone packages:

```
sudo apt update

sudo apt install -y keystone
```

This above command installs the Keystone service along with its dependencies.

Configure Keystone Database

Keystone requires a database to store its data, including users, roles, and service catalogs. MySQL (MariaDB) is typically used for this purpose. First, create a database for Keystone:

```
sudo mysql -u root -p
```

Once logged into MySQL, execute the following commands to create the database and grant appropriate permissions:

```
CREATE DATABASE keystone;

GRANT ALL PRIVILEGES ON keystone.* TO
'keystone'@'localhost' IDENTIFIED BY 'StrongPassword';

GRANT ALL PRIVILEGES ON keystone.* TO 'keystone'@'%'
IDENTIFIED BY 'StrongPassword';

FLUSH PRIVILEGES;

EXIT;
```

Next, populate the Keystone database by running the migration script:

```
sudo keystone-manage db_sync
```

This command initializes the Keystone database schema.

Configure Keystone

Now, configure the Keystone service by editing the **keystone.conf** file located in **/etc/keystone/keystone.conf**. For this, start by setting up the database connection:

```
[database]

connection =
mysql+pymysql://keystone:StrongPassword@controller/keysto
ne
```

Next, configure the **token** provider. The **fernet** token format is recommended for its simplicity and security:

```
[token]
```

```
provider = fernet
```

Save the file and exit the editor.

Initialize Fernet Keys

Fernet tokens require a key repository to encrypt and decrypt tokens. Initialize the Fernet key repository using the following command:

```
sudo keystone-manage fernet_setup --keystone-user
keystone --keystone-group keystone

sudo keystone-manage credential_setup --keystone-user
keystone --keystone-group keystone
```

This step creates the necessary keys and sets up the repository.

Bootstrap Keystone

Next, bootstrap Keystone to create the initial configuration for the service:

```
sudo keystone-manage bootstrap --bootstrap-password
StrongPassword \

    --bootstrap-admin-url http://controller:5000/v3/ \

    --bootstrap-internal-url http://controller:5000/v3/ \

    --bootstrap-public-url http://controller:5000/v3/ \

    --bootstrap-region-id RegionOne
```

Configure Apache HTTP Server

Now, Keystone runs behind the Apache HTTP server, which acts as a proxy and provides SSL termination if needed. Here, enable the Apache **wsgi** module and restart the service:

```
sudo apt install -y apache2 libapache2-mod-wsgi-py3
```

```
sudo service apache2 restart
```

This command ensures that Apache is set up to handle requests to Keystone.

Verify Keystone Installation

After the installation, verify that Keystone is functioning correctly by exporting the admin credentials:

```
export OS_USERNAME=admin

export OS_PASSWORD=StrongPassword

export OS_PROJECT_NAME=admin

export OS_USER_DOMAIN_NAME=Default

export OS_PROJECT_DOMAIN_NAME=Default

export OS_AUTH_URL=http://controller:5000/v3

export OS_IDENTITY_API_VERSION=3
```

Now, issue a command to request a token:

```
openstack token issue
```

If the command returns a token, Keystone is successfully installed and operational.

Create Keystone Domain, Projects, Users, and Roles

Now that Keystone is up and running, you can begin setting up your identity management structure. Start by creating a domain, a project, a user, and assigning a role:

```
openstack domain create --description "Default Domain"
default

openstack project create --domain default --description
"Admin Project" admin
```

```
openstack user create --domain default --password-prompt
admin

openstack role create admin

openstack role add --project admin --user admin admin
```

Repeat these above commands to create additional projects, users, and roles as needed.

Populate the Service Catalog

Finally, populate the Keystone service catalog with the available OpenStack services. Each service requires an entry in the service catalog so that it can be discovered by other OpenStack components. For example, to register the Keystone service itself:

```
openstack service create --name keystone --description
"OpenStack Identity" identity

openstack endpoint create --region RegionOne identity
public http://controller:5000/v3

openstack endpoint create --region RegionOne identity
internal http://controller:5000/v3

openstack endpoint create --region RegionOne identity
admin http://controller:5000/v3
```

Now, follow the similar steps as above to register other services like Glance, Nova, and Neutron in the catalog. With Keystone in place, GitforGits can confidently proceed to deploy and manage the other OpenStack components.

Recipe 4: Installing and Configuring Glance

Glance Overview

Glance is the image service within the OpenStack ecosystem, responsible for the discovery, registration, and retrieval of virtual machine images. These images are the templates or "blueprints" from which instances (virtual machines) are created. Glance is a central repository that stores these images and provides them to other OpenStack services like Nova (Compute) when launching instances. Images managed by Glance can be bare-metal images, virtual machine snapshots, or custom-built images tailored to specific application needs. The service also supports various storage backends, including local file systems, object storage (like Swift), and external storage systems (like Ceph).

Glance assists GitforGits by:

- It offers a single point of control for managing all virtual machine images used within the cloud, ensuring consistency and standardization across the environment.

- Glance supports multiple image formats, such as QCOW2, RAW, VHD, and VMDK, allowing users to work with different hypervisors and virtualization technologies.

- Glance allows you to manage different versions of images, making it easier to track updates and roll back if necessary. It also supports extensive metadata management, enabling detailed descriptions and categorizations of images.

- Glance seamlessly integrates with Nova, Cinder, and other OpenStack services, ensuring that images are readily available for launching instances or attaching to volumes.

Now, let's walk through the process of installing and configuring Glance on your system running the OpenStack Bobcat.

Install Glance Packages

Here, start by installing the Glance service on your controller node. The Glance package includes both the API server and the image registry:

```
sudo apt update

sudo apt install -y glance
```

This command installs the Glance service and its necessary dependencies.

Configure Glance Database

Glance requires a database to store image metadata. Similar to Keystone, Glance uses MySQL (MariaDB) for this purpose. Begin by creating the Glance database:

```
sudo mysql -u root -p
```

Once logged into MySQL, execute the following commands to create the Glance database and grant the necessary permissions:

```
CREATE DATABASE glance;
```

```
GRANT ALL PRIVILEGES ON glance.* TO 'glance'@'localhost'
IDENTIFIED BY 'StrongPassword';

GRANT ALL PRIVILEGES ON glance.* TO 'glance'@'%'
IDENTIFIED BY 'StrongPassword';

FLUSH PRIVILEGES;

EXIT;
```

Next, synchronize the Glance database by running the migration script:

```
sudo glance-manage db_sync
```

This command initializes the Glance database schema.

Configure Glance

Then, configure the Glance service by editing the **glance-api.conf** file located in **/etc/glance/glance-api.conf**. Start by setting up the database connection:

```
[database]

connection =
mysql+pymysql://glance:StrongPassword@controller/glance
```

And, configure the **keystone** authentication settings to allow Glance to authenticate with the Keystone service:

```
[keystone_authtoken]

auth_url = http://controller:5000/v3

memcached_servers = controller:11211

auth_type = password

project_domain_name = Default
```

```
user_domain_name = Default

project_name = service

username = glance

password = StrongPassword
```

Here, specify the storage backend which Glance will use to store images. For simplicity, we'll use the local file system:

```
[glance_store]

stores = file,http

default_store = file

filesystem_store_datadir = /var/lib/glance/images/
```

Ensure that the **filesystem_store_datadir** directory is correctly set up to store images. And the, save the file and exit the editor.

Register Glance with Keystone

To allow other OpenStack services to discover and use Glance, register the Glance service in Keystone's service catalog.

First, begin by creating the Glance user:

```
openstack user create --domain default --password-prompt glance
```

Assign the **admin** role to the Glance user in the **service** project:

```
openstack role add --project service --user glance admin
```

Create the Glance service entry:

```
openstack service create --name glance --description
"OpenStack Image" image
```

Finally, create the public, internal, and admin endpoints for the Glance API:

```
openstack endpoint create --region RegionOne image public
http://controller:9292
```

```
openstack endpoint create --region RegionOne image
internal http://controller:9292
```

```
openstack endpoint create --region RegionOne image admin
http://controller:9292
```

These above commands register Glance in the Keystone service catalog, making it available to other OpenStack components.

Start the Glance Services

With the above configuration complete, then you may start the Glance services and ensure they are enabled to start automatically on boot:

```
sudo systemctl enable glance-api
```

```
sudo systemctl start glance-api
```

These above commands start the Glance API service, which will listen for requests to manage images. Now after this, to ensure that Glance is working correctly, verify the installation by listing the available images (though none will be present initially):

```
openstack image list
```

The command should return an empty list, indicating that Glance is operational and ready to manage images.

Uploading an Image to Glance

Alright. So now we will upload a sample image to verify that Glance can store and manage images. You can use the CirrOS image, a minimal Linux distribution commonly used for testing available to download from the following URL:

http://download.cirros-cloud.net/0.5.2/cirros-0.5.2-x86_64-disk.img

```
curl -O http://download.cirros-cloud.net/0.5.2/cirros-
0.5.2-x86_64-disk.img
```

```
openstack image create "CirrOS" --file cirros-0.5.2-
x86_64-disk.img --disk-format qcow2 --container-format
bare --public
```

This command downloads the CirrOS image and uploads it to Glance. After the upload is complete, list the images again:

```
openstack image list
```

The CirrOS image should now appear in the list, confirming that Glance is properly configured and functional.

Managing Image Metadata

Glance allows you to manage extensive metadata for each image, which can include properties like architecture, OS type, and more. You can view the metadata for an image using:

```
openstack image show "CirrOS"
```

To add or modify metadata, use the **--property** flag. For example, to specify that this image is 64-bit:

```
openstack image set --property architecture=x86_64
"CirrOS"
```

The above management of the metadata helps in categorizing and selecting images based on specific criteria, which is particularly useful in large environments. With this, Glance is now integrated with Keystone for authentication, and images can be stored, retrieved, and managed through the OpenStack interface.

Recipe 5: Installing and Configuring Neutron

Purpose of Neutron

Neutron is the networking component of OpenStack, responsible for providing "Networking as a Service" (NaaS) between interface devices managed by other OpenStack services like Nova. Neutron offers a powerful, flexible, and scalable networking solution that allows cloud administrators to define and manage networks, subnets, routers, and other networking services such as firewalls, VPNs, and load balancers. In a cloud environment, neutron provides the tools to achieve this by abstracting the underlying network infrastructure, allowing for complex topologies and advanced networking features, such as:

- Neutron handles both Layer 2 (data link layer) networking, such as VLANs and VXLANs, and Layer 3 (network layer) functions, including routing and NAT.
- Neutron enables administrators to define and apply security policies at the network level through security groups and firewall rules.
- Neutron allows instances to be assigned public IP addresses (floating IPs), enabling external access.
- Through the use of VLANs, VXLANs, or GRE tunnels, Neutron can segment networks to isolate traffic between different tenants or projects.

Let's get into the step-by-step process of installing and configuring Neutron:

Install Neutron Packages

Neutron is composed of several components that need to be installed. Here, you begin by installing the core Neutron services on the controller node as below:

```
sudo apt update

sudo apt install -y neutron-server neutron-plugin-ml2
neutron-linuxbridge-agent neutron-dhcp-agent neutron-
metadata-agent neutron-l3-agent
```

This command installs the Neutron server, the Modular Layer 2 (ML2) plugin, and agents required for DHCP, metadata, and Layer 3 (routing) services.

Configure the Neutron Database

Neutron requires a database to store networking information. Create the Neutron database in MySQL (MariaDB):

```
sudo mysql -u root -p
```

Once logged into MySQL, create the database and grant permissions:

```
CREATE DATABASE neutron;

GRANT ALL PRIVILEGES ON neutron.* TO
'neutron'@'localhost' IDENTIFIED BY 'StrongPassword';

GRANT ALL PRIVILEGES ON neutron.* TO 'neutron'@'%'
IDENTIFIED BY 'StrongPassword';

FLUSH PRIVILEGES;

EXIT;
```

Next, synchronize the Neutron database schema:

```
sudo neutron-db-manage --config-file
/etc/neutron/neutron.conf --config-file
/etc/neutron/plugins/ml2/ml2_conf.ini upgrade head
```

This command initializes the Neutron database with the required tables.

Configure Neutron

Neutron configuration involves multiple files. We'll start with the main configuration in **neutron.conf**, located in **/etc/neutron/neutron.conf**. Begin by setting up the database connection:

```
[database]

connection =
mysql+pymysql://neutron:StrongPassword@controller/neutron
```

Next, configure Neutron to authenticate with Keystone:

```
[keystone_authtoken]

auth_uri = http://controller:5000
```

```
auth_url = http://controller:5000

memcached_servers = controller:11211

auth_type = password

project_domain_name = Default

user_domain_name = Default

project_name = service

username = neutron

password = StrongPassword
```

Neutron will use the ML2 plugin for managing Layer 2 networking. Next, configure the ML2 plugin by editing the **ml2_conf.ini** file located in **/etc/neutron/plugins/ml2/ml2_conf.ini**:

```
[ml2]

type_drivers = flat,vlan,vxlan

tenant_network_types = vxlan

mechanism_drivers = linuxbridge,l2population

extension_drivers = port_security


[ml2_type_flat]

flat_networks = provider


[ml2_type_vxlan]

vni_ranges = 1:1000
```

```
[securitygroup]

enable_security_group = True

firewall_driver = iptables
```

This configuration enables flat and VLAN provider networks, as well as VXLAN tenant networks. The Linux Bridge can be used as the mechanism driver, which is a common choice for simple networking setups.

Configure Linux Bridge Agent

The Linux Bridge agent handles Layer 2 networking and needs to be configured to work with your physical network interfaces. Edit the **linuxbridge_agent.ini** file located in **/etc/neutron/plugins/ml2/linuxbridge_agent.ini**:

```
[linux_bridge]

physical_interface_mappings = provider:eth1


[vxlan]

enable_vxlan = True

local_ip = 10.0.0.11

l2_population = True


[securitygroup]

enable_security_group = True

firewall_driver = iptables
```

Here, replace **eth1** with the physical network interface that is connected to your provider network. The **local_ip** should be set to the IP address of the management interface on the compute node.

Configure the DHCP Agent

The DHCP agent is responsible for assigning IP addresses to instances. Edit the **dhcp_agent.ini** file located in **/etc/neutron/dhcp_agent.ini**:

```
[DEFAULT]

interface_driver = linuxbridge

dhcp_driver = neutron.agent.linux.dhcp.Dnsmasq

enable_isolated_metadata = True
```

This above configuration sets the interface driver to Linux Bridge and uses Dnsmasq as the DHCP driver.

Configure the Metadata Agent

The metadata agent allows instances to retrieve instance-specific data, such as SSH keys and user data. Configure the **metadata_agent.ini** file located in **/etc/neutron/metadata_agent.ini**:

```
[DEFAULT]

nova_metadata_host = controller

metadata_proxy_shared_secret = StrongSecret
```

The **nova_metadata_host** should point to the controller node, and **metadata_proxy_shared_secret** is a shared secret that should match the configuration in Nova.

Configure the L3 Agent

The L3 agent handles routing and NAT for instances. Configure the **l3_agent.ini** file located in **/etc/neutron/l3_agent.ini**:

```
[DEFAULT]
```

```
interface_driver = linuxbridge
```

This simple configuration ensures that the L3 agent uses the Linux Bridge interface driver for routing.

Register Neutron with Keystone

To allow other OpenStack services to discover and use Neutron, register the Neutron service in Keystone's service catalog. To do this, start by creating the Neutron user:

```
openstack user create --domain default --password-prompt
neutron
```

Assign the **admin** role to the Neutron user in the **service** project:

```
openstack role add --project service --user neutron admin
```

Create the Neutron service entry:

```
openstack service create --name neutron --description
"OpenStack Networking" network
```

Finally, create the public, internal, and admin endpoints for the Neutron API:

```
openstack endpoint create --region RegionOne network
public http://controller:9696
```

```
openstack endpoint create --region RegionOne network
internal http://controller:9696
```

```
openstack endpoint create --region RegionOne network
admin http://controller:9696
```

These above commands register Neutron in the Keystone service catalog, making it available to other OpenStack components.

Start the Neutron Services

With the configuration complete, start the Neutron services and ensure they are enabled to start automatically on boot:

```
sudo systemctl restart neutron-server neutron-
linuxbridge-agent neutron-dhcp-agent neutron-metadata-
agent neutron-l3-agent
```

```
sudo systemctl enable neutron-server neutron-linuxbridge-
agent neutron-dhcp-agent neutron-metadata-agent neutron-
l3-agent
```

These commands start the Neutron services, which will handle all networking operations within OpenStack. To ensure that Neutron is working correctly, verify the installation by checking the network agents:

```
openstack network agent list
```

The command should return a list of agents, all of which should be in the **UP** state, indicating that Neutron is properly configured and operational.

Creating a Network and Subnet

Let's create a sample network and subnet to verify that Neutron is functioning as expected. Start by creating a network:

```
openstack network create --share --provider-network-type
flat --provider-physical-network provider provider
```

Next, create a subnet on this network:

```
openstack subnet create --network provider --allocation-
pool start=192.168.1.100,end=192.168.1.200 --dns-
nameserver 8.8.8.8 --gateway 192.168.1.1 --subnet-range
192.168.1.0/24 provider-subnet
```

This command creates a subnet on the provider network with the specified IP range and DNS settings.

With the above outlined directions, Neutron is now ready to manage networks, subnets, and advanced networking features, such that instances can communicate securely and efficiently across the cloud.

Recipe 6: Installing and Configuring Nova

Nova's Characteristics

Nova is the core compute service within OpenStack, managing the lifecycle of virtual machines (VMs) or instances. It orchestrates everything from launching instances, managing resources (like CPU, memory, and storage), to handling the shutdown and deletion of instances. Nova interfaces with other OpenStack services like Glance for retrieving VM images, Neutron for networking, and Cinder for block storage. Nova's primary function is to provision and manage virtualized compute resources on demand. It supports various hypervisors, including KVM, QEMU, and VMware, offering flexibility in how the compute infrastructure is deployed. Nova abstracts the complexities of managing virtualized environments, allowing cloud administrators to efficiently scale compute resources as needed.

For GitforGits, deploying and configuring Nova is essential for providing scalable and manageable compute resources. Now, let's walk through the process of installing and configuring Nova on your Ubuntu system running the OpenStack Bobcat release.

Installing and Configuring Nova

Let us begin by installing the Nova services on the controller node. It consists of several components that need to be installed and configured:

```
sudo apt update

sudo apt install -y nova-api nova-conductor nova-
scheduler nova-novncproxy nova-consoleauth
```

This command installs the Nova API, conductor, scheduler, console proxy, and console authentication services.

Configure the Nova Database

Nova also requires a database to store information about instances, flavors, and other compute-related resources. And so we can do the same creating the Nova and Nova API databases in MySQL:

```
sudo mysql -u root -p
```

Once logged into MySQL, create the databases and grant the necessary permissions:

```
CREATE DATABASE nova;

CREATE DATABASE nova_api;

GRANT ALL PRIVILEGES ON nova.* TO 'nova'@'localhost'
IDENTIFIED BY 'StrongPassword';

GRANT ALL PRIVILEGES ON nova.* TO 'nova'@'%' IDENTIFIED
BY 'StrongPassword';

GRANT ALL PRIVILEGES ON nova_api.* TO 'nova'@'localhost'
IDENTIFIED BY 'StrongPassword';

GRANT ALL PRIVILEGES ON nova_api.* TO 'nova'@'%'
IDENTIFIED BY 'StrongPassword';

FLUSH PRIVILEGES;

EXIT;
```

Next, synchronize the Nova database schema by running the migration scripts:

```
sudo nova-manage db sync
```

This command initializes the Nova and Nova API databases with the required tables.

Configure Nova

Now, configure the Nova service by editing the **nova.conf** file located in **/etc/nova/nova.conf**. Start by setting up the database connections:

```
[api_database]

connection =
mysql+pymysql://nova:StrongPassword@controller/nova_api
```

```
[database]

connection =
mysql+pymysql://nova:StrongPassword@controller/nova
```

Next, configure Nova to authenticate with Keystone:

```
[keystone_authtoken]

auth_uri = http://controller:5000

auth_url = http://controller:5000

memcached_servers = controller:11211

auth_type = password

project_domain_name = Default

user_domain_name = Default

project_name = service

username = nova

password = StrongPassword
```

Specify the transport URL for messaging between Nova services:

```
[DEFAULT]

transport_url =
rabbit://openstack:StrongPassword@controller
```

Finally, configure the VNC proxy settings to enable console access to instances:

```
[vnc]
```

```
enabled = True

vncserver_listen = $my_ip

vncserver_proxyclient_address = $my_ip

novncproxy_base_url =
http://controller:6080/vnc_auto.html
```

Ensure to replace **$my_ip** with the IP address of your controller node and then save and exit the editor.

Configure Nova Compute Service

If you are running a separate compute node, you will need to install and configure the Nova compute service on that node. So first, begin by installing the compute service:

```
sudo apt update

sudo apt install -y nova-compute
```

On the compute node, edit the **nova.conf** file to point to the appropriate database and messaging service on the controller node. For example:

```
[DEFAULT]

transport_url =
rabbit://openstack:StrongPassword@controller

my_ip = 10.0.0.21


[api_database]

connection =
mysql+pymysql://nova:StrongPassword@controller/nova_api
```

```
[database]
```

```
connection =
mysql+pymysql://nova:StrongPassword@controller/nova
```

Additionally, configure the compute node to use the correct hypervisor. For KVM, the default, ensure the following settings are in place:

```
[libvirt]
```

```
virt_type = kvm
```

After configuring the compute node, restart the Nova compute service:

```
sudo systemctl restart nova-compute
```

Register Nova with Keystone

To allow other OpenStack services to discover and use Nova, register the Nova service in Keystone's service catalog. Start by creating the Nova user:

```
openstack user create --domain default --password-prompt
nova
```

Assign the **admin** role to the Nova user in the **service** project:

```
openstack role add --project service --user nova admin
```

Create the Nova service entry:

```
openstack service create --name nova --description
"OpenStack Compute" compute
```

Finally, create the public, internal, and admin endpoints for the Nova API:

```
openstack endpoint create --region RegionOne compute
public http://controller:8774/v2.1
```

```
openstack endpoint create --region RegionOne compute
internal http://controller:8774/v2.1

openstack endpoint create --region RegionOne compute
admin http://controller:8774/v2.1
```

These above commands register Nova in the Keystone service catalog, making it available to other OpenStack components.

Start Nova Services

With the configuration complete, start the Nova services on the controller node and ensure they are enabled to start automatically on boot:

```
sudo systemctl restart nova-api nova-scheduler nova-
conductor nova-novncproxy nova-consoleauth

sudo systemctl enable nova-api nova-scheduler nova-
conductor nova-novncproxy nova-consoleauth
```

These commands start the Nova services, which will handle all compute operations within OpenStack.

Create a Flavor

Flavors define the compute, memory, and storage capacity of instances in OpenStack. To create a standard flavor for GitforGits, use the following command:

```
openstack flavor create --id 1 --vcpus 2 --ram 2048 --
disk 20 m1.small
```

This command creates a flavor named **m1.small** with 2 virtual CPUs, 2 GB of RAM, and 20 GB of disk space.

Launch an Instance

Now let's launch a test instance to verify that Nova can deploy virtual machines. Use the CirrOS image that was uploaded to Glance in the previous recipe:

```
openstack server create --flavor m1.small --image CirrOS
--nic net-id=$(openstack network list -f value -c ID) --
security-group default --key-name mykey test-instance
```

This command launches an instance named **test-instance** using the **m1.small** flavor, the CirrOS image, and a key pair named **mykey**.

Accessing Instance Console

To access the console of the launched instance, use the following command:

```
openstack console url show test-instance
```

This command returns a URL that you can open in a web browser to access the instance's console, verifying that the VNC proxy is configured correctly. With this, Nova is now ready to manage compute resources, launch instances, and scale workloads dynamically based on demand.

Recipe 7: Setting up Cinder for Block Storage

Block Storage and Volume Service

Block storage is a type of storage that provides persistent data storage by emulating a physical hard drive. Unlike object storage, which stores data as discrete objects, block storage breaks data into fixed-sized chunks (blocks) and stores them individually. Each block has its unique identifier, and the storage system can retrieve blocks independently, making block storage highly efficient for databases, virtual machines, and applications requiring quick access to structured data.

In OpenStack, block storage is managed by the Cinder service. Cinder provides a robust and scalable way to create, attach, and manage block storage volumes that can be used by instances (VMs) in Nova. These volumes can be attached to running instances, allowing them to store data persistently even after the instance is terminated. This is especially important for applications that require consistent, long-term storage, such as databases, transaction logs, or any application data that needs to survive a reboot or instance termination.

Cinder supports a wide range of backend storage solutions, including traditional hard drives, SSDs, and distributed storage systems like Ceph. It also offers advanced features such as snapshots, backups, and volume replication, for maintaining data integrity and availability in enterprise environments.

Introduction to Cinder

Cinder is the block storage component of OpenStack. It is designed to manage the lifecycle of block storage volumes, providing users with a flexible and reliable way to manage persistent storage. Cinder integrates seamlessly with Nova, allowing instances to attach and use block storage volumes just like physical disks.

The key functionalities of Cinder:

- Create, delete, attach, and detach volumes to/from instances.
- Take snapshots of volumes to preserve the state of the data at a particular point in time.
- Create backups of volumes to ensure data safety and recoverability.
- Replicate volumes across different storage backends for high availability and disaster recovery.
- Configure multiple storage backends, such as LVM, Ceph, NFS, or enterprise SANs, to provide different types of storage.

Whether it's for storing databases, application logs, or any other persistent data, Cinder ensures that the data is securely stored and easily accessible by the instances running in the cloud.

Installing and Configuring Cinder

Now, let's go through the process of installing and configuring Cinder. The Cinder comprises several components that need to be installed on the controller node.

Let us begin by installing the necessary Cinder services:

```
sudo apt update

sudo apt install -y cinder-api cinder-scheduler
```

This command installs the Cinder API and scheduler services, which are responsible for handling API requests and scheduling volume creation and management tasks.

Configure Cinder Database

Similar to what we have done so far, the Cinder requires database to store information about volumes, snapshots, and backups and for this we will create the Cinder database in MySQL:

```
sudo mysql -u root -p
```

Once logged into MySQL, create the Cinder database and grant the necessary permissions:

```
CREATE DATABASE cinder;
```

```
GRANT ALL PRIVILEGES ON cinder.* TO 'cinder'@'localhost'
IDENTIFIED BY 'StrongPassword';

GRANT ALL PRIVILEGES ON cinder.* TO 'cinder'@'%'
IDENTIFIED BY 'StrongPassword';

FLUSH PRIVILEGES;

EXIT;
```

Next, synchronize the Cinder database schema by running the migration script:

```
sudo cinder-manage db sync
```

This command initializes the Cinder database with the required tables.

Configure Cinder

Now, configure the Cinder service by editing the **cinder.conf** file located in **/etc/cinder/cinder.conf**. Start by setting up the database connection:

```
[database]

connection =
mysql+pymysql://cinder:StrongPassword@controller/cinder
```

Next, configure Cinder to authenticate with Keystone:

```
[keystone_authtoken]

auth_uri = http://controller:5000

auth_url = http://controller:5000

memcached_servers = controller:11211

auth_type = password

project_domain_name = Default
```

```
user_domain_name = Default

project_name = service

username = cinder

password = StrongPassword
```

Specify the transport URL for messaging between Cinder services:

```
[DEFAULT]

transport_url =
rabbit://openstack:StrongPassword@controller
```

Finally, configure the storage backend. For this example, we'll use the default LVM (Logical Volume Manager) backend. Add the following to the **cinder.conf** file:

```
[lvm]

volume_driver = cinder.volume.drivers.lvm.LVMVolumeDriver

volume_group = cinder-volumes

iscsi_protocol = iscsi

iscsi_helper = tgtadm


[DEFAULT]

enabled_backends = lvm

default_volume_type = lvm
```

And finally, save the file and exit the editor.

Prepare LVM Backend

If you're using LVM as the backend, you'll need to set up a volume group that Cinder can use to create volumes:

```
sudo pvcreate /dev/sdb
```

Replace **/dev/sdb** with the appropriate disk or partition that you intend to use for Cinder volumes.

Next, create a volume group named **cinder-volumes**:

```
sudo vgcreate cinder-volumes /dev/sdb
```

This volume group will be used by Cinder to create logical volumes for block storage.

Register Cinder with Keystone

To allow other OpenStack services to discover and use Cinder, register the Cinder service in Keystone's service catalog:

```
openstack user create --domain default --password-prompt
cinder
```

Assign the **admin** role to the Cinder user in the **service** project:

```
openstack role add --project service --user cinder admin
```

Create the Cinder service entry:

```
openstack service create --name cinder --description
"OpenStack Block Storage" volume

openstack service create --name cinderv2 --description
"OpenStack Block Storage" volumev2

openstack service create --name cinderv3 --description
"OpenStack Block Storage" volumev3
```

Finally, create the public, internal, and admin endpoints for the Cinder API:

```
openstack endpoint create --region RegionOne volume
public http://controller:8776/v1/%(tenant_id)s

openstack endpoint create --region RegionOne volume
internal http://controller:8776/v1/%(tenant_id)s

openstack endpoint create --region RegionOne volume admin
http://controller:8776/v1/%(tenant_id)s

openstack endpoint create --region RegionOne volumev2
public http://controller:8776/v2/%(tenant_id)s

openstack endpoint create --region RegionOne volumev2
internal http://controller:8776/v2/%(tenant_id)s

openstack endpoint create --region RegionOne volumev2
admin http://controller:8776/v2/%(tenant_id)s

openstack endpoint create --region RegionOne volumev3
public http://controller:8776/v3/%(tenant_id)s

openstack endpoint create --region RegionOne volumev3
internal http://controller:8776/v3/%(tenant_id)s

openstack endpoint create --region RegionOne volumev3
admin http://controller:8776/v3/%(tenant_id)s
```

And these above listed commands register Cinder in the Keystone service catalog, thereby making it available to other OpenStack components.

Start Cinder Services

Now with the configuration complete, we can start the Cinder services and are enabled to start automatically on boot:

```
sudo systemctl enable cinder-scheduler cinder-api

sudo systemctl start cinder-scheduler cinder-api
```

If you have configured Cinder to use LVM on the controller or a separate storage node, start the volume service as well:

```
sudo systemctl enable cinder-volume
```

```
sudo systemctl start cinder-volume
```

These commands start the Cinder services, which will handle all block storage operations within OpenStack. And, to ensure that Cinder is working correctly, verify the installation by listing the available volumes (though none will be present initially):

```
openstack volume list
```

The command should return an empty list, indicating that Cinder is operational and ready to manage block storage volumes.

Creating and Attaching a Volume

Let's create a test volume to verify that Cinder can manage block storage. Use the following command to create a 1 GB volume:

```
openstack volume create --size 1 test-volume
```

After the volume is created, attach it to an existing instance:

```
openstack server add volume test-instance test-volume
```

This command attaches the **test-volume** to the **test-instance** launched in the previous recipe.

Accessing the Volume from the Instance

To verify that the volume is accessible from the instance, log into the instance and list the available disks:

```
lsblk
```

You should see the **test-volume** listed as an additional disk attached to the instance. You can now format and mount the volume within the instance, making it available for use. With Cinder in place, GitforGits can efficiently manage the storage needs of their applications, ensuring data persistence and availability across their cloud environment.

Recipe 8: Defining Network Topology for OpenStack

Understanding Network Topology

Network topology refers to the arrangement of various elements (links, nodes, etc.) within a computer network. In an OpenStack environment, defining a network topology ensures that instances (VMs) can communicate with each other, access external networks, and interact with other OpenStack services like Neutron (networking), Nova (compute), and Cinder (block storage).

For GitforGits, a well-planned network topology ensures efficient traffic management, secure communication between services, and the ability to scale as the company grows. The right network topology will involve the design and implementation of several network components, such as management networks, tenant networks, and external networks, each serving a distinct purpose in the cloud environment.

Choosing the Right Network Topology

Given the needs of GitforGits, which likely include development, testing, and production environments, the following network topology suits the best fit:

Management Network

This network handles internal OpenStack communication between services, such as Neutron, Nova, Cinder, and Keystone. It's essential for the operation of the OpenStack control plane and should be isolated from other networks to enhance security.

Tenant Network

These are the networks created for the instances running in the cloud. Each tenant (or project) can have its own network, which is isolated from other tenants. These networks can be flat, VLAN, or VXLAN-based, depending on the scalability and security requirements.

External (Public) Network

This network allows instances to communicate with the outside world. Instances can be assigned floating IPs from this network to make them accessible from the internet.

Storage Network

This optional network is dedicated to block storage traffic between Cinder and the compute nodes. Separating storage traffic helps in optimizing performance by preventing it from interfering with other network traffic.

This above topology provides a clear separation of different types of traffic, which improves security, performance, and manageability. We will now walk through the steps to define and implement this topology in OpenStack.

Now, let's define and set up this network topology in your OpenStack Bobcat environment.

Define Management Network

The management network is the backbone of the OpenStack control plane. It should be configured first to ensure that all OpenStack services can communicate effectively.

Create Management Network

```
openstack network create --share --provider-network-type
flat --provider-physical-network provider mgmt-net
```

This command creates a flat network called **mgmt-net** that will be used for internal communication between OpenStack services.

Create Management Subnet

```
openstack subnet create --network mgmt-net --subnet-range
10.0.0.0/24 --gateway 10.0.0.1 --dns-nameserver 8.8.8.8
mgmt-subnet
```

This creates a subnet on the **mgmt-net** network with the specified IP range. The management network should be isolated from the tenant and external networks to prevent unauthorized access to the control plane.

Define Tenant Network

The tenant network is where the instances will be deployed. This network is isolated from the management network and other tenants' networks.

- Create Tenant Network

```
openstack network create tenant-net
```

This command creates a network called **tenant-net** that will be used for tenant instances.

- Create Tenant Subnet

```
openstack subnet create --network tenant-net --subnet-
range 192.168.10.0/24 --gateway 192.168.10.1 --dns-
nameserver 8.8.8.8 tenant-subnet
```

This creates a subnet on the **tenant-net** network with the specified IP range. Each tenant can have its own network with isolated subnets.

- Create Router to Connect Tenant Networks to External

```
openstack router create tenant-router

openstack router set tenant-router --external-gateway
ext-net

openstack router add subnet tenant-router tenant-subnet
```

This creates a router named **tenant-router**, sets its external gateway to **ext-net** (external network), and connects the tenant subnet to this router. This setup allows instances in the tenant network to access external networks, including the internet.

Define External Network

The external network is where floating IPs are allocated, allowing instances to be accessible from outside the OpenStack environment.

- Create External Network

```
openstack network create --external --provider-network-
type flat --provider-physical-network provider ext-net
```

This command creates a flat external network named **ext-net**.

- Create External Subnet

```
openstack subnet create --network ext-net --subnet-range
203.0.113.0/24 --allocation-pool
start=203.0.113.100,end=203.0.113.200 --dns-nameserver
8.8.8.8 --gateway 203.0.113.1 ext-subnet
```

This creates a subnet on the **ext-net** network with a specific IP range for floating IPs. Instances in the tenant network can be assigned floating IPs from this range to make them accessible from the public internet.

Assign Floating IPs to Instances

Once the networks are set up, you can assign floating IPs to instances to make them accessible from outside the OpenStack environment:

- Allocate a Floating IP

```
openstack floating ip create ext-net
```

This command allocates a floating IP from the **ext-net** network.

- Associate the Floating IP with an Instance

```
openstack server add floating ip test-instance
203.0.113.101
```

Replace **test-instance** with the name of your instance and **203.0.113.101** with the floating IP you allocated. This makes the instance accessible from the public network.

Security Groups and Firewall Rules

To secure the network, define security groups and firewall rules to control the traffic allowed to and from the instances:

- Create a Security Group

```
openstack security group create web-servers --description
"Security group for web servers"
```

This command creates a security group named **web-servers**.

- Define Ingress Rules

```
openstack security group rule create --protocol tcp --
dst-port 22 --remote-ip 0.0.0.0/0 web-servers
```

```
openstack security group rule create --protocol tcp --
dst-port 80 --remote-ip 0.0.0.0/0 web-servers
```

These commands allow incoming SSH (port 22) and HTTP (port 80) traffic to instances in the **web-servers** security group.

- Assign the Security Group to an Instance

```
openstack server add security group test-instance web-
servers
```

This assigns the **web-servers** security group to the **test-instance**, ensuring that only allowed traffic can reach the instance.

This above topology includes a management network for internal communication, tenant networks for isolated instance communication, an external network for public access, and an optional storage network for dedicated storage traffic.

Summary

To conclude, we looked at the fundamentals of configuring an OpenStack infrastructure for GitforGits. First, we configured the hardware and verified that the Linux environment was ready for OpenStack deployment. Next, we discussed how to install and configure Keystone, the identity service required by all OpenStack components to handle authentication and authorization. After that, Glance was configured and installed, making it simple to manage virtual machine images. It was explained in detail how to configure Neutron with the primary goal of creating a robust networking environment capable of handling both internal and external communications in the cloud infrastructure. Nova was then configured to manage computing resources, enabling the creation and management of virtual machine instances. Cinder was created to provide persistent block storage, ensuring that data could be kept secure and easily managed.

Finally, we designed and implemented a network topology tailored specifically for GitforGits. This provided us with a clear way to manage traffic, ensure communication security, and allow people outside of GitforGits to access cloud resources. Each step builds on the previous one, resulting in a fully functional and scalable OpenStack environment. By following these steps, we established a solid foundation for the cloud environment and ensured that all prime services were up and running. This enabled the OpenStack framework to grow and become more flexible in the future.

CHAPTER 2: IDENTITY MANAGEMENT WITH KEYSTONE

Introduction

Here in this chapter, we will focus on Keystone, the identity management service in OpenStack for controlling access and ensuring security across the cloud environment. Although we installed Keystone in the previous chapter, this chapter will delve deeper into its configuration and management, equipping you with the necessary skills to fully utilize its capabilities. We will explore how Keystone handles tokens, which are vital for authenticating and authorizing requests within OpenStack. You will also learn how to set up RBAC policies, which are essential for defining who can access specific resources and what actions they can perform. Additionally, we will cover the configuration and use of the Service Catalog, which aids in managing and discovering the various services within your OpenStack environment.

Further, this chapter will teach you how to integrate Keystone with LDAP for centralized user management, implementing multi-domain support for managing multiple organizations or environments within the same OpenStack deployment, and using Keystone Federation to enable authentication across multiple clouds. Finally, we will address common issues that may arise with Keystone and provide troubleshooting strategies to resolve them effectively. By the end of this chapter, you will be able to manage the identity and access within your OpenStack environment for enabling secure and efficient operations.

Recipe 1: Managing Keystone Tokens

Understanding Keystone Tokens

Keystone tokens are essential components in the OpenStack identity service. They are used to authenticate and authorize requests across different OpenStack services. When a user or service requests access to an OpenStack resource, Keystone issues a token that represents the user's credentials and the permissions they have been granted. This token is then used by the client (user or service) to access OpenStack APIs without having to repeatedly authenticate with username and password.

There are several types of tokens in Keystone, with **Fernet tokens** being the most commonly used in recent OpenStack deployments due to their security and efficiency. Unlike older token types (such as UUID tokens), Fernet tokens are lightweight, stateless, and do not require persistent storage, making them ideal for large-scale deployments. These tokens are cryptographically signed and can only be decrypted by Keystone, ensuring that the information they contain remains secure.

Fernet tokens typically have a limited lifespan, after which they expire and must be renewed. This expiration is a key security feature, reducing the risk of token misuse if a token were to be intercepted. Keystone also manages the lifecycle of tokens, including their creation, validation, and revocation. Understanding how to manage these tokens for maintaining the security and efficiency of your OpenStack environment is vital to us.

Now, let's dive into the practical aspects of managing Keystone tokens, focusing on Fernet tokens, which are likely the default in our OpenStack Bobcat environment.

Viewing Token Information

To view details about a specific token, you can use the OpenStack command-line interface (CLI). First, ensure you have an active token by authenticating with Keystone:

```
openstack token issue
```

This command will generate a token and display details such as the token ID, expiration time, and the associated user and project.

Validating a Token

To check whether a token is valid (i.e., it has not expired or been revoked), use the following command:

```
openstack token show <token_id>
```

If the token is valid, Keystone will return its details; if it has expired or been revoked, an error message will be displayed.

Revoking a Token

Revoking a token invalidates it before its natural expiration, preventing it from being used to access resources. This is particularly useful if a security issue is suspected. To revoke a token, use the following command:

```
openstack token revoke <token_id>
```

After revocation, any further attempts to use this token will fail.

Managing Fernet Keys

These Fernet tokens rely on a set of cryptographic keys managed by Keystone. These keys are rotated periodically to enhance security. The key repository typically resides in **/etc/keystone/fernet-keys**. To manually rotate the keys, use the following command:

```
sudo keystone-manage fernet_rotate
```

Here, key rotation ensures that old tokens can be invalidated while maintaining the validity of current tokens. Keystone manages key rotation automatically, but it's important to understand how to perform this task manually if needed.

Checking Token Expiration Settings

Token expiration settings balance security and usability. By default, tokens have a relatively short lifespan to minimize the window in which a stolen token could be used. To check the current expiration settings, inspect the Keystone configuration file (**/etc/keystone/keystone.conf**):

```
[token]

expiration = 3600
```

This setting indicates that tokens will expire 3600 seconds (or 1 hour) after they are issued. Adjust this setting as needed based on your security policies.

Auditing and Token Usage

The auditing of token usage can be useful for security and compliance purposes. By enabling token auditing, you can track when and how tokens are used within your environment. To enable token auditing, you would typically configure logging settings in the **keystone.conf** file.

For example:

```
[token]

provider = fernet

expiration = 3600

revocation_cache_time = 3600

audit_log = /var/log/keystone/keystone_token_audit.log
```

This setup not only tracks token usage but also ensures that audit logs are stored for future reference.

Through this recipe, we learned to issue, validate, revoke, and audit tokens, focusing on the use of Fernet tokens for their enhanced security features. Also, we covered the importance of key rotation and how to adjust token expiration settings to suit your organization's security needs.

Recipe 2: Setting up RBAC Policies

RBAC in OpenStack

RBAC is a fundamental security mechanism in OpenStack to control who can perform specific actions on resources within the cloud environment. RBAC works by assigning roles to users, and each role defines a set of permissions that determine what actions a user can take. These roles are often project-specific, meaning that a user might have different roles in different projects, thus limiting or granting access based on the context.

RBAC manages access to resources across various departments or teams. For instance, developers might need access to certain compute resources within their project, but not have the ability to modify networking configurations. Conversely, network administrators might have full control over Neutron services but limited access to compute resources.

Let's walk through the process of setting up a basic RBAC policy in OpenStack for GitforGits, and then explore how this policy can be applied or limited to specific projects.

Defining Roles

First, let's define a set of roles that match the needs of GitforGits. We'll create a custom role named **developer** that will have limited access to certain OpenStack services, and another role named **network-admin** with broader access to network-related resources.

- Create the **developer** Role

```
openstack role create developer
```

This command creates a role named **developer**.

- Create the **network-admin** Role

```
openstack role create network-admin
```

This command creates a role named **network-admin**. Both these roles are now available to be assigned to users within specific projects.

Assigning Roles to Users

Once roles are defined, they need to be assigned to users within a project. This assignment determines what each user can do within that project.

- Assign the **developer** Role to a User

Let's assign the **developer** role to a user named **alice** in a project named **dev-project:**

```
openstack role add --project dev-project --user alice
developer
```

This command grants Alice the **developer** role within the **dev-project**, giving her the permissions associated with that role.

- Assign the **network-admin** Role to a User

Similarly, assign the **network-admin** role to a user named **bob** in a project named **network-project**

```
openstack role add --project network-project --user bob
network-admin
```

Bob now has the **network-admin** role within the **network-project**, allowing him to manage network resources within that project.

Creating and Applying RBAC Policies

RBAC policies in OpenStack are generally defined in a policy file, typically located at **/etc/keystone/policy.json** or **/etc/keystone/policy.yaml**. These files define the permissions associated with each role for various OpenStack services.

- Editing the Policy File

To create custom policies, you would modify the **policy.json** or **policy.yaml** file. For example, to restrict the **developer** role from deleting instances, you might add a policy like this:

```
"compute:delete": "role:admin or role:network-admin"
```

This line ensures that only users with the **admin** or **network-admin** roles can delete instances, while those with the **developer** role cannot.

- Applying the Policy

After editing the policy file, restart the Keystone service to apply the changes:

```
sudo systemctl restart keystone
```

The new policies are now in effect, and users will be limited by the permissions defined in these policies.

Applying RBAC to Specific Projects

RBAC policies can be applied differently across projects, allowing for fine-grained control over who can do what in each project. Suppose you want the **developer** role to have full access to resources in the **dev-project** but restricted access in another project, say **prod-project**. You can create different roles or modify the policy to be project-specific.

In the **dev-project**, Alice (with the **developer** role) might have permissions to launch instances:

```
"compute:start": "role:developer and
project_id:%(project_id)s"
```

But in the **prod-project**, you might limit this to:

```
"compute:start": "role:developer and
project_id:%(project_id)s and project_name:dev-project"
```

This policy ensures that Alice can start instances only in the **dev-project** and not in **prod-project**.

Verifying RBAC Implementation

To verify that the RBAC policies are working as expected, attempt to perform actions as a user with different roles.

- Testing the **developer** Role

Log in as Alice and try to delete an instance in **dev-project**. The command should fail if the policy is correctly applied:

```
openstack server delete <instance_id>
```

This should return a permission error, confirming that the **developer** role does not have delete permissions.

- Testing the **network-admin** Role

Log in as Bob and try to create a network in **network-project**. The command should succeed, confirming that the **network-admin** role has the necessary permissions:

```
openstack network create test-network
```

If the network is created, the RBAC policy is working as intended.

Through this recipe, we defined custom roles like **developer** and **network-admin**, assigned these roles to users within specific projects, and demonstrated how to enforce and verify RBAC policies using OpenStack's policy files.

Recipe 3: Configuring and Utilizing Service Catalog

Understanding the Service Catalog

The Service Catalog in OpenStack is a vital component managed by Keystone, providing a directory of all available services in the cloud environment and their associated endpoints. It acts as a centralized registry, allowing users and other services to discover and interact with OpenStack components like Nova (Compute), Glance (Image Service), Neutron (Networking), and Cinder (Block Storage). Each service listed in the catalog is associated with one or more endpoints, which are URLs that point to the specific network addresses where the services can be accessed.

There are typically three types of endpoints in a service catalog:

Public Endpoint: This endpoint is accessible from outside the cloud environment. It's usually used by external users or applications that interact with OpenStack services over the internet or a public network.

Internal Endpoint: This endpoint is used for internal communication within the OpenStack environment. It's not exposed to the external world, making it more secure for internal service-to-service interactions.

Admin Endpoint: This endpoint is used for administrative tasks and is usually restricted to administrators. It typically offers broader access to manage and configure services.

For GitforGits, a company managing a growing cloud infrastructure, the internal and admin endpoints secure internal operations and management, while the public endpoint is important for making certain services available to external users or customers. A well-configured service catalog ensures that all services are discoverable and accessible based on their intended use, providing a seamless experience for both administrators and users.

Now, with the given GitforGits' requirements, the service catalog should be configured to clearly separate the internal, public, and admin endpoints, ensuring secure and efficient access. The internal endpoint will be used for communication between OpenStack services, the admin endpoint for administrative tasks, and the public endpoint for external access where necessary. With this, let's learn to configure this service catalog in your OpenStack environment.

Define Services in the Catalog

Each service in OpenStack must be registered in the service catalog. We'll start by ensuring that core services like Nova, Glance, Neutron, and Cinder are properly registered.

- Register the Compute (Nova) Service

```
openstack service create --name nova --description
"OpenStack Compute" compute
```

This command registers the Nova service with the type **compute** in the service catalog.

- Register the Image (Glance) Service

```
openstack service create --name glance --description
"OpenStack Image Service" image
```

This registers the Glance service with the type **image**.

- Register the Networking (Neutron) Service

```
openstack service create --name neutron --description
"OpenStack Networking Service" network
```

This registers the Neutron service with the type **network**.

- Register the Block Storage (Cinder) Service

```
openstack service create --name cinder --description
"OpenStack Block Storage" volume

openstack service create --name cinderv2 --description
"OpenStack Block Storage v2" volumev2
```

```
openstack service create --name cinderv3 --description
"OpenStack Block Storage v3" volumev3
```

These commands register the Cinder service with types **volume**, **volumev2**, and **volumev3** for different API versions.

Define Endpoints for each Service

After the services are registered, endpoints must be created to make these services accessible. We'll create public, internal, and admin endpoints for each service.

- Create Endpoints for the Compute (Nova) Service

```
openstack endpoint create --region RegionOne compute
public http://controller:8774/v2.1

openstack endpoint create --region RegionOne compute
internal http://controller:8774/v2.1

openstack endpoint create --region RegionOne compute
admin http://controller:8774/v2.1
```

These commands create the public, internal, and admin endpoints for the Nova service.

- Create Endpoints for the Image (Glance) Service

```
openstack endpoint create --region RegionOne image public
http://controller:9292

openstack endpoint create --region RegionOne image
internal http://controller:9292

openstack endpoint create --region RegionOne image admin
http://controller:9292
```

These commands create the endpoints for the Glance service.

- Create Endpoints for the Networking (Neutron) Service

```
openstack endpoint create --region RegionOne network
public http://controller:9696
```

```
openstack endpoint create --region RegionOne network
internal http://controller:9696
```

```
openstack endpoint create --region RegionOne network
admin http://controller:9696
```

These commands create the endpoints for the Neutron service.

- Create Endpoints for the Block Storage (Cinder) Service

```
openstack endpoint create --region RegionOne volume
public http://controller:8776/v1/%(tenant_id)s
```

```
openstack endpoint create --region RegionOne volume
internal http://controller:8776/v1/%(tenant_id)s
```

```
openstack endpoint create --region RegionOne volume admin
http://controller:8776/v1/%(tenant_id)s
```

```
openstack endpoint create --region RegionOne volumev2
public http://controller:8776/v2/%(tenant_id)s
```

```
openstack endpoint create --region RegionOne volumev2
internal http://controller:8776/v2/%(tenant_id)s
```

```
openstack endpoint create --region RegionOne volumev2
admin http://controller:8776/v2/%(tenant_id)s
```

```
openstack endpoint create --region RegionOne volumev3
public http://controller:8776/v3/%(tenant_id)s
```

```
openstack endpoint create --region RegionOne volumev3
internal http://controller:8776/v3/%(tenant_id)s

openstack endpoint create --region RegionOne volumev3
admin http://controller:8776/v3/%(tenant_id)s
```

These commands create the endpoints for all versions of the Cinder service.

Verifying the Service Catalog

After configuring the service catalog, it's important to verify that all services are correctly registered and that their endpoints are accessible.

- List All Services in the Catalog

To see a list of all registered services, use:

```
openstack service list
```

This command displays all the services that have been registered with their names and types.

- List All Endpoints

To verify that the endpoints have been created correctly, use:

```
openstack endpoint list
```

This command displays all the endpoints along with their associated services, URLs, and regions.

Testing Endpoint Accessibility

You can test the accessibility of a specific service endpoint using a curl command. For example, to test the public endpoint of the Nova service:

```
curl http://controller:8774/v2.1
```

If the service is up and running, you should receive a response, typically an error message related to authentication, indicating that the service is accessible.

By properly setting up the service catalog, GitforGits ensures that all OpenStack components are discoverable and accessible based on their intended use, whether for internal operations, public access, or administrative tasks. This structured approach enhances security and manageability to efficiently operate its cloud infrastructure.

Recipe 4: Integrating Keystone with LDAP

Role of LDAP

Lightweight Directory Access Protocol (LDAP) is a protocol used to access and manage directory information over a network. LDAP is widely used for authenticating and authorizing users across various systems, making it a central component in many enterprise environments. By integrating OpenStack's Keystone with an existing LDAP directory, GitforGits can centralize user management, reduce administrative overhead, and maintain consistency in user authentication across multiple platforms.

LDAP integration allows Keystone to authenticate users against an existing directory service, such as Microsoft Active Directory (AD) or OpenLDAP, instead of managing a separate user database. This approach is particularly beneficial for large organizations that already have an established LDAP infrastructure, as it simplifies user management by leveraging the existing directory.

Benefits of LDAP Integration

- **Centralized User Management**: LDAP allows all user accounts to be managed in one place, ensuring consistency and reducing duplication of effort.
- **Single Sign-On (SSO)**: Users can use their existing LDAP credentials to access OpenStack, reducing the need for multiple passwords.
- **Scalability**: LDAP is designed to handle large numbers of users and can scale easily with the organization's needs.
- **Security**: Integrating with LDAP ensures that authentication policies, such as password complexity and expiration rules, are consistent across all platforms.

For GitforGits, integrating Keystone with LDAP will streamline identity management, providing a unified user experience and enhancing security by aligning with existing enterprise authentication protocols.

Now, let's walk through the process of configuring Keystone to use LDAP as its backend for identity management.

Configuring LDAP in Keystone

- Edit the Keystone Configuration File

The Keystone configuration file (**/etc/keystone/keystone.conf**) needs to be updated to use LDAP as the identity backend. Open the file in a text editor:

```
sudo nano /etc/keystone/keystone.conf
```

- Configure the Identity Driver

In the **[identity]** section, set the driver to **ldap**:

```
[identity]

driver = keystone.identity.backends.ldap.Identity
```

- Configure the LDAP Connection

In the **[ldap]** section, configure the connection details to your LDAP server. Here's an example configuration:

```
[ldap]

url = ldap://ldap.example.com

user = cn=admin,dc=example,dc=com

password = LDAPAdminPassword

suffix = dc=example,dc=com

user_tree_dn = ou=users,dc=example,dc=com

user_objectclass = inetOrgPerson

user_id_attribute = cn

user_name_attribute = cn

user_mail_attribute = mail

user_enabled_attribute = userAccountControl

user_enabled_mask = 2

user_enabled_default = 512
```

```
user_enabled_invert = True
```

Replace **ldap.example.com** with the address of your LDAP server, and **LDAPAdminPassword** with the LDAP administrator password. The **suffix** refers to the base DN for your LDAP directory, and **user_tree_dn** points to the subtree where user accounts are stored.

- Mapping LDAP Groups to Keystone Roles

If you want to map LDAP groups to Keystone roles, add the following configuration:

```
role_tree_dn = ou=groups,dc=example,dc=com

role_objectclass = groupOfNames

role_id_attribute = cn

role_name_attribute = cn

role_member_attribute = member
```

This configuration maps LDAP groups located under **ou=groups,dc=example,dc=com** to Keystone roles.

Configuring Keystone to use LDAP Backend

- Synchronize the LDAP Directory with Keystone

After configuring the LDAP connection, sync the LDAP directory with Keystone to ensure that the directory structure is compatible:

```
sudo keystone-manage db_sync
```

This command updates Keystone's database to reflect the LDAP backend configuration.

- Restart the Keystone Service

Restart the Keystone service to apply the changes:

```
sudo systemctl restart keystone
```

Creating LDAP Users and Assigning Roles

Once LDAP is integrated with Keystone, you can create users and assign roles to them directly from the LDAP directory.

- Creating an LDAP User

Create a new user in your LDAP directory. This can be done using an LDAP management tool like **ldapadd** or through an interface provided by your LDAP server (e.g., Active Directory Users and Computers for AD).

- Assigning a Role to an LDAP User in Keystone

After the user is created in LDAP, assign a role to them in Keystone:

```
openstack role add --project dev-project --user
<LDAP_username> developer
```

Replace **<LDAP_username>** with the username of the LDAP user. This command assigns the **developer** role to the user within the **dev-project** in OpenStack.

Verifying LDAP Integration

- Testing User Authentication

Test the LDAP integration by attempting to authenticate with an LDAP user:

```
openstack token issue --os-username <LDAP_username> --os-
password <LDAP_password> --os-auth-url
http://controller:5000/v3 --os-project-name dev-project -
-os-user-domain-name Default --os-project-domain-name
Default
```

If the configuration is correct, Keystone will issue a token for the user, indicating successful authentication.

- Checking User Roles

Verify that the user has been assigned the correct roles by listing their roles within the project:

```
openstack role list --project dev-project --user
<LDAP_username>
```

This command should display the roles assigned to the LDAP user within the specified project.

Through this recipe, we configured Keystone to use LDAP as its backend, synchronized the LDAP directory with Keystone, and demonstrated how to create LDAP users and assign roles to them in OpenStack.

Recipe 5: Implementing Multi-Domain Support

Need for Multi-Domain Support

As organizations grow and expand, their infrastructure needs become increasingly complex. For GitforGits, which may have different departments, teams, or even separate business units, managing identity and access across a single domain might become limiting and difficult to scale. This is where multi-domain support in Keystone becomes essential.

Now, why Multi-Domain Support is important for GitforGits:

- **Separation of Concerns**: Multi-domain support allows GitforGits to isolate and manage users, projects, and roles across different domains, ensuring that each department or business unit can operate independently while still being managed under a single OpenStack deployment. This separation is particularly useful for organizations that have multiple environments, such as development, testing, and production, or for those that manage different customer environments.

- **Enhanced Security and Compliance**: By separating users and resources into different domains, GitforGits can enforce stricter access controls, ensure data segregation, and comply with industry-specific regulations. For example, if GitforGits handles sensitive data that needs to be isolated by law or internal policies, multi-domain support ensures that data remains within its designated domain, preventing unauthorized access from other parts of the organization.

- **Scalability and Flexibility**: As GitforGits expands, adding new teams, departments, or even geographical locations, multi-domain support allows the organization to scale its identity management without affecting existing configurations. New domains can be created for each new business unit or location, providing the flexibility to grow without compromising the overall structure.

Enabling Multi-Domain Support

- Edit the Keystone Configuration File

Open the Keystone configuration file (**/etc/keystone/keystone.conf**) and ensure that the following options are set to enable multi-domain support:

```
[identity]

driver = keystone.identity.backends.sql.Identity


[assignment]

driver = keystone.assignment.backends.sql.Assignment
```

These settings ensure that Keystone uses SQL backends for identity and assignment, which support multi-domain configurations.

- Restart Keystone

After updating the configuration, restart the Keystone service to apply the changes:

```
sudo systemctl restart keystone
```

Creating a New Domain

With multi-domain support enabled, you can now create new domains to segregate users, projects, and roles.

- Create a New Domain

Let's create a new domain for the **Research** department within GitforGits:

```
openstack domain create --description "Research
Department Domain" research-domain
```

This command creates a domain named **research-domain** with a description indicating that it's for the Research department.

- Verify the Domain Creation

To ensure that the domain has been created successfully, list all available domains:

```
openstack domain list
```

The output should include **research-domain** along with the default domain.

Creating Users and Projects within New Domain

Next, create users and projects that are specific to the **research-domain**.

- Create a Project within the New Domain

Create a project named **research-project** under the **research-domain**:

```
openstack project create --domain research-domain --
description "Project for Research Department" research-
project
```

This command creates a project named **research-project** within the **research-domain**.

- Create a User within the New Domain

Create a user named **researcher1** within the **research-domain**:

```
openstack user create --domain research-domain --
password-prompt researcher1
```

This command creates a user named **researcher1** and prompts for a password. The user is associated with the **research-domain**.

- Assign a Role to the User within the Project

Assign the **member** role to **researcher1** within the **research-project**:

```
openstack role add --project research-project --user
researcher1 member
```

This command assigns the **member** role to **researcher1** for the **research-project** within the **research-domain**.

Managing and Accessing Multiple Domains

With multiple domains in place, users must specify their domain when authenticating to ensure they access the correct resources.

- Authenticating as a User in a Specific Domain

To authenticate as **researcher1** in the **research-domain**, use the following command:

```
openstack token issue --os-username researcher1 --os-
password <password> --os-domain-name research-domain --
os-auth-url http://controller:5000/v3
```

- Listing Projects

After authenticating, list the projects accessible to **researcher1**:

```
openstack project list --domain research-domain
```

This command should list the **research-project**, confirming that the user is correctly associated with the domain and project.

Managing Roles Across Domains

Multi-domain support allows for roles to be managed independently across domains, ensuring that permissions can be customized according to the needs of each department.

- Create a Custom Role for the New Domain

Suppose the Research department requires a special role, **research-admin**, with elevated privileges. Create this role:

```
openstack role create research-admin
```

This role can now be assigned to users within the **research-domain** as needed.

- Assign the Custom Role

Assign the **research-admin** role to a user within the **research-domain**:

```
openstack role add --project research-project --user
researcher1 research-admin
```

This command assigns the **research-admin** role to **researcher1** within the **research-project**.

Through this recipe, we enabled multi-domain support, created a new domain, set up users and projects within that domain, and explored how to manage roles across domains. This capability maintains separation of resources, enforcing security policies, and scaling the identity management system as the organization grows.

Recipe 6: Using Keystone Federation for Multi-Cloud Authentication

Understanding Keystone Federation

Keystone Federation in OpenStack is a powerful feature that enables identity sharing across multiple OpenStack clouds or between OpenStack and other identity providers. Essentially, it allows users to authenticate in one cloud (or identity provider) and gain access to resources in another cloud without needing separate credentials for each environment. This capability is particularly useful in hybrid or multi-cloud scenarios, where GitforGits might use multiple cloud environments to optimize their operations.

Federation relies on establishing trust relationships between different identity providers (IdPs) and service providers (SPs). In a federated setup, Keystone acts as the service provider, while an external identity provider (which could be another Keystone instance or a completely different system like an enterprise SSO) handles user authentication. Once authenticated, the user's identity is asserted across the different clouds or environments, allowing seamless access to resources.

Necessity of Multi-Cloud Authentication

For a growing organization which might leverage different cloud environments for various purposes—such as public clouds for scalable workloads, private clouds for sensitive data, or even different OpenStack clouds for regional operations—managing multiple identities and credentials can become complex and cumbersome. Multi-cloud authentication through Keystone Federation simplifies this by allowing GitforGits to:

- **Unified Identity Management**: Users can authenticate once using their primary credentials and access resources across multiple clouds, reducing the need for managing multiple sets of credentials.

- **Improved Security**: Federation ensures that sensitive credentials are not spread across multiple clouds. Instead, authentication is handled by a trusted identity provider, and only temporary, scoped access tokens are shared between environments.

- **Operational Efficiency**: By streamlining access across clouds, GitforGits can ensure that their teams can efficiently move workloads or data between environments without facing authentication barriers.

Now, let's walk through the process of configuring Keystone Federation to enable multi-cloud authentication in your OpenStack environment.

Setting up the Identity Provider (IdP)

In this example, we will assume that GitforGits has two OpenStack environments: a primary environment (acting as the Identity Provider) and a secondary environment (acting as the Service Provider).

- Configure the Identity Provider

On the primary OpenStack environment (the IdP), you need to configure Keystone to act as the identity provider. Edit the Keystone configuration file (**/etc/keystone/keystone.conf**):

```
[federation]

remote_id_attribute = HTTP_OIDC_ISS
```

This configuration sets up the attribute that will be used to identify users authenticated via federation.

- Create the Identity Provider in Keystone

Register the Identity Provider with Keystone:

```
openstack identity provider create --remote-id
http://idp.example.com idp
```

Replace **http://idp.example.com** with the actual URL of the identity provider. The **idp** is a name identifier for the Identity Provider in your Keystone setup.

- Create a Mapping for the Identity Provider

Mappings define how incoming federated assertions (user attributes) are translated into local Keystone user identities. Create a mapping for the IdP:

```
openstack mapping create --rules '[

{

    "local": [

        {

            "user": {

                "name": "{0}",
```

```
                    "domain": {
                            "name": "Default"
                    }
            }
        },
        {
            "group": {
                "name": "federated_users",
                "domain": {
                        "name": "Default"
                }
            }
        }
    ],
    "remote": [
        {
            "type": "openstack_user"
        }
    ]
}
]' idp_mapping
```

This mapping associates federated users with a local domain and user group in Keystone.

- Associate the Mapping with the Identity Provider

Associate the **idp_mapping** with the Identity Provider:

```
openstack identity provider set --mapping idp_mapping idp
```

This completes the setup on the Identity Provider side.

Setting up Service Provider (SP)

Next, configure the secondary OpenStack environment to act as a Service Provider that will trust the Identity Provider.

- Register the Service Provider in the Identity Provider

On the IdP environment, create a service provider entry that represents the SP:

```
openstack service provider create --auth-url
https://sp.example.com/v3/OS-
FEDERATION/identity_providers/idp/protocols/saml2/auth --
service-provider-url
https://sp.example.com/Shibboleth.sso/SAML2/POST sp
```

Replace **https://sp.example.com** with the actual URL of the service provider. This tells the IdP how to communicate with the SP.

- Configure the Service Provider

On the SP environment, configure Keystone to recognize and trust the Identity Provider. Edit the Keystone configuration file on the SP (**/etc/keystone/keystone.conf**):

```
[federation]

trusted_dashboard = https://sp.example.com/dashboard


[auth]

methods = external,password,token,oauth1,saml2
```

This configuration ensures that the SP accepts authentication from the IdP.

- Create a Protocol for the Service Provider

On the SP, register the protocol (e.g., SAML2) used for federated authentication:

```
openstack federation protocol create --identity-provider
idp --mapping idp_mapping saml2
```

This links the **saml2** protocol with the Identity Provider and the mapping that was created earlier.

Federating Users Across Clouds

Now that the Identity Provider and Service Provider are set up, users can authenticate with the IdP and access resources in the SP.

- Create Federated Roles

On both the IdP and SP, create roles that will be used for federated users. For example, create a role named **federated_user**:

```
openstack role create federated_user
```

This role will be assigned to federated users to grant them specific permissions.

- Assign Federated Roles to Users

Assign the **federated_user** role to a user in the SP:

```
openstack role add --user <user_name> --project
<project_name> federated_user
```

Replace **<user_name>** and **<project_name>** with the actual user and project names. This allows the federated user to access the project resources in the SP environment.

This setup is particularly valuable in multi-cloud scenarios, where the organization leverages various cloud environments for different purposes. Through this recipe, we configured Keystone to act as both an Identity Provider and a Service Provider, established trust relationships between these environments, and demonstrated how users can authenticate and access resources across clouds using federated identity. This capability enhances security, simplifies user management, and increases operational efficiency for GitforGits as it continues to expand its cloud infrastructure.

Recipe 7: Troubleshooting Common Keystone Issues

Understanding Common Keystone Issues

While implementing Keystone for identity management, as detailed in Recipes 1 through 7, several challenges and errors might arise. These issues can range from configuration mistakes to more complex problems related to service integration, authentication failures, and federation. Understanding the potential pitfalls and how to troubleshoot them effectively maintains a robust and secure OpenStack environment.

Here, we'll go through the most common issues that you might encounter while configuring and managing Keystone, and provide practical troubleshooting tips, expert practices, and hacks to help resolve these issues efficiently.

Keystone Service Fails to Start

One of the most common issues is that the Keystone service fails to start after initial configuration or after changes have been made. This can be due to incorrect configuration files, missing dependencies, or problems with the underlying database.

Troubleshooting Tips

Check Configuration Files

The first step is to check the **/etc/keystone/keystone.conf** file for any syntax errors or incorrect settings. Use tools like **cat** or **less** to inspect the file and ensure that all settings are correctly configured.

```
cat /etc/keystone/keystone.conf
```

- Verify Database Connection

Keystone relies heavily on its database. Make sure that the database settings in the **[database]** section of **keystone.conf** are correct, and that the database is accessible. Test the connection to the database using a command like:

```
mysql -u keystone -p -h controller
```

If the database connection fails, check the credentials and network accessibility between Keystone and the database server.

Inspect Logs

Keystone logs are invaluable for diagnosing issues. Check the logs located in **/var/log/keystone/keystone.log** for any error messages or stack traces that indicate why the service failed to start.

```
tail -f /var/log/keystone/keystone.log
```

- Restart the Service

After making changes, restart the Keystone service and monitor the logs to see if the issue persists:

```
sudo systemctl restart keystone
```

Authentication Failures

Users are unable to authenticate with Keystone, resulting in errors like "Invalid user/password" or "Could not find token."

Troubleshooting Tips

- Validate Credentials

Ensure that the user credentials (username, password, domain, and project) are correct. Use the OpenStack CLI to manually issue a token and check if the credentials are valid:

```
openstack token issue --os-username <username> --os-
password <password> --os-project-name <project_name> --
os-auth-url http://controller:5000/v3
```

If the token is issued successfully, the credentials are correct.

Check Keystone Logs

Authentication issues are often logged in the Keystone logs. Look for errors related to authentication failures, such as incorrect credentials or missing roles.

```
grep -i "authentication" /var/log/keystone/keystone.log
```

- Verify User and Role Configuration

Ensure that the user is correctly assigned to the appropriate roles and projects. Use the OpenStack CLI to list roles and verify user assignments:

```
openstack role list --user <username> --project
<project_name>
```

Check Token Expiry

If tokens are being issued but authentication fails later, check the token expiration settings in the **keystone.conf** file. Tokens that expire too quickly might cause unexpected authentication failures.

```
[token]

expiration = 3600  # 1 hour
```

Consider extending the token expiration time if this is the cause.

Token Validation Issues

Keystone fails to validate tokens, often resulting in errors like "Token not found" or "Invalid token."

Troubleshooting Tips

- Ensure Proper Token Management

If you're using Fernet tokens, ensure that the key repository is properly managed. Verify that the key files in **/etc/keystone/fernet-keys/** are intact and have the correct permissions.

```
ls -l /etc/keystone/fernet-keys/
```

- Rotate Fernet Keys

If token validation issues persist, consider rotating the Fernet keys. This can help resolve issues related to corrupted keys or synchronization problems between Keystone nodes.

```
sudo keystone-manage fernet_rotate
```

After rotation, ensure that the key distribution mechanism (e.g., rsync) is correctly synchronizing the keys across all Keystone nodes.

- Check Token Cache

If you're using a caching mechanism like Memcached, ensure that the cache is functioning properly. Issues with the token cache can cause validation failures. Restart Memcached to clear any stale cache entries:

```
sudo systemctl restart memcached
```

Federation Configuration Issues

Federation setup between Identity Providers (IdPs) and Service Providers (SPs) fails, leading to issues like "Federated authentication not working" or "Cannot find federated user."

Troubleshooting Tips

- Verify IdP and SP Configuration

Ensure that both the IdP and SP are correctly configured. This includes setting up the federation mappings and protocols in Keystone. Double-check the configuration files and the entries in the Keystone database.

```
openstack federation protocol list --identity-provider
<idp>
```

- Check SAML Assertions

If you're using SAML2 for federation, inspect the SAML assertions being exchanged between the IdP and SP. Use a tool like **SAML Tracer** (a browser extension) to capture and analyze the SAML assertions.

- Sync Time Between IdP and SP

Time synchronization is a key in a federated setup. Ensure that both the IdP and SP have their clocks synchronized using NTP. If the clocks are out of sync, token validation might fail.

```
sudo systemctl restart ntp
```

- Inspect Apache and Keystone Logs

Since federated authentication often involves Apache (for handling SAML2), inspect both the Apache logs (**/var/log/apache2/**) and the Keystone logs for any errors related to federation.

```
tail -f /var/log/apache2/error.log
```

LDAP Integration Issues

Keystone fails to authenticate users against an LDAP directory, leading to errors like "LDAP connection failed" or "User not found in LDAP."

Troubleshooting Tips

Verify LDAP Connectivity

Ensure that Keystone can connect to the LDAP server. Use tools like **ldapsearch** to test the connection and query the LDAP directory from the Keystone node.

```
ldapsearch -x -H ldap://ldap.example.com -D
"cn=admin,dc=example,dc=com" -W -b
"ou=users,dc=example,dc=com"
```

If the connection fails, check the network connectivity, LDAP server status, and credentials.

Check LDAP Configuration

Review the LDAP settings in the **keystone.conf** file. Ensure that the **url**, **user**, **password**, **user_tree_dn**, and other relevant fields are correctly configured.

```
[ldap]

url = ldap://ldap.example.com

user = cn=admin,dc=example,dc=com

password = LDAPAdminPassword

user_tree_dn = ou=users,dc=example,dc=com
```

- Inspect Keystone Logs for LDAP Errors

Keystone logs often provide detailed information about LDAP-related issues. Look for LDAP-specific errors in the logs:

```
grep -i "ldap" /var/log/keystone/keystone.log
```

Ensure Proper SSL/TLS Configuration

If you're using LDAPS (LDAP over SSL), ensure that SSL/TLS is correctly configured and that the Keystone node trusts the LDAP server's certificate. Update the **keystone.conf** file with the correct certificate paths if necessary.

```
[ldap]

use_tls = True

tls_cacertfile = /etc/ssl/certs/ca-certificates.crt
```

RBAC Issues

Users with certain roles are unable to perform actions that they should have permission to do, leading to errors like "Unauthorized action" or "Access denied."

Troubleshooting Tips

- Verify Role Assignments

Ensure that the user has been assigned the correct roles within the appropriate project or domain. Use the following command to check role assignments:

```
openstack role assignment list --user <username> --
project <project_name>
```

Check Policy Files

Keystone uses policy files to enforce RBAC. Ensure that the **policy.json** or **policy.yaml** file is correctly configured, and that the permissions for the roles are as intended.

```
cat /etc/keystone/policy.json
```

- Refresh Policy Cache

If you've made changes to the policy file, you might need to clear Keystone's policy cache to apply the changes:

```
sudo keystone-manage token_flush

sudo systemctl restart keystone
```

- Use Debug Mode

Enable debug mode in the **keystone.conf** file to get more detailed logging information, which can help in diagnosing RBAC issues:

```
[DEFAULT]

debug = True
```

After enabling debug mode, restart Keystone and review the logs for detailed error messages.

Issues with Multi-Domain Support

Users or projects in different domains cannot access resources as expected, or domain-specific roles and permissions are not functioning correctly.

Troubleshooting Tips

Ensure Domain-Specific Configuration

Verify that domain-specific settings are correctly configured in **keystone.conf**, and that users and projects are correctly associated with their respective domains.

```
openstack user list --domain <domain_name>
```

Check Domain Mappings

If you're using custom mappings for multi-domain support, ensure that the mappings are correctly defined and associated with the appropriate domains.

```
openstack mapping list
```

- Inspect Logs for Domain-Related Issues

Look for errors related to domain configuration or access in the Keystone logs:

```
grep -i "domain" /var/log/keystone/keystone.log
```

- Test Domain-Specific Authentication

Test authentication for users in different domains to ensure that domain-specific configurations are working as expected:

```
openstack token issue --os-username <username> --os-
password <password> --os-project-name <project_name> --
os-domain-name <domain_name> --os-auth-url
http://controller:5000/v3
```

Service Catalog Issues

Services fail to appear in the service catalog, or endpoints are not accessible, leading to errors like "Service not found" or "Endpoint unreachable."

Troubleshooting Tips

- Check Service and Endpoint Registration

Verify that the services and their endpoints are correctly registered in the service catalog:

```
openstack service list

openstack endpoint list
```

Ensure that the endpoints have the correct URLs and are associated with the correct regions.

- Test Endpoint Accessibility

Use **curl** or similar tools to test the accessibility of service endpoints directly:

```
curl http://controller:8774/v2.1   # For Nova API
```

If the endpoint is not accessible, check the service configuration and network settings.

- Inspect Keystone Logs for Service Catalog Errors

Look for any errors related to the service catalog in the Keystone logs:

```
grep -i "service catalog" /var/log/keystone/keystone.log
```

In this recipe, we've covered the most common Keystone issues—from service startup failures to authentication problems, token validation issues, federation configuration challenges, LDAP integration, RBAC issues, multi-domain support problems, and service catalog errors. By following the expert practices, smart techniques, and troubleshooting tips provided, likewise GitforGits, you can also effectively maintain a robust Keystone setup, ensuring that identity management and access control remain secure and efficient across its OpenStack environment.

Summary

To summarize, the focus of this chapter was on mastering identity management within OpenStack using Keystone. The chapter began by exploring Keystone tokens, understanding their purpose, and learning how to manage them effectively. This included issuing, validating, revoking, and rotating tokens, which are essential for maintaining secure and efficient authentication processes. Next, the concept of RBAC was introduced, where roles were created and assigned to users within specific projects, ensuring that access to resources was appropriately controlled. The chapter then covered the configuration and use of the Service Catalog, emphasizing how to register services and define endpoints to ensure proper service discovery and access.

We also detailed the integration of Keystone with LDAP, which enables centralized user management by utilizing existing LDAP directories. We also discussed the necessity and implementation of multi-domain support in Keystone, emphasizing its role in managing separate organizational units within the same OpenStack deployment. Finally, the chapter delved into Keystone Federation, demonstrating how it enables multi-cloud authentication by establishing trust between different clouds or identity providers. The chapter concluded with troubleshooting common Keystone issues, providing practical tips and solutions to resolve and prevent problems that may arise during Keystone implementation and management. Through these topics, GitforGits gained a comprehensive understanding of how to effectively manage identity and access control within their OpenStack environment.

CHAPTER 3: IMAGE MANAGEMENT WITH GLANCE

Introduction

Glance is the service that stores, discovers, and retrieves virtual machine images in OpenStack. In Chapter 3, we will explore this aspect of image management. Previously, we focused on setting up the OpenStack infrastructure and managing identity via Keystone; in this chapter, we will learn how to efficiently manage images for deploying instances across your cloud environment. You'll learn how to create and register images in Glance, ensuring that the appropriate templates are available for your virtual machines. We will also go over how to create custom images with Cloud-Init, which allows for the automated configuration of instances at launch.

To help you better organize and retrieve images, we will go over how to manage their metadata and properties. You'll also learn to configure Glance for various storage backends, such as Swift and Ceph, to optimize image storage and access. The chapter will also cover how to automate image uploads with the Glance CLI, making it easier to manage images at scale. We'll look at how to manage image versions and updates so that your instances always use the most current and secure images. Finally, we'll talk about how to secure and encrypt images in Glance for staying compliant with security standards.

Recipe 1: Creating and Registering Images in Glance

Introduction to Image Management

Glance is the OpenStack Image Service, which provides services for discovering, registering, and retrieving virtual machine images. These images serve as templates from which instances are created. Efficient image management ensures the availability of right configurations and operating systems for deployment across your cloud environment. In this recipe, we will walk through the process of creating and registering images in Glance, a fundamental step in preparing your OpenStack environment for instance deployment.

Before we can create and register images, we must ensure that the Glance CLI is installed and configured properly. The Glance CLI is a powerful tool that allows you to interact with the Glance service directly from the command line, making image management tasks more efficient and easier to automate.

Installing Glance CLI

The Glance CLI is part of the OpenStack client package. If you have already installed the OpenStack client on your system, the Glance CLI should be available. If not, you can install it by following these steps:

- Update Your Package List

Begin by updating the package list on your Ubuntu system:

```
sudo apt update
```

- Install the OpenStack Client

Install the OpenStack client, which includes the Glance CLI:

```
sudo apt install -y python3-openstackclient
```

- Verify Installation

To verify that the Glance CLI is installed, you can check the version of the OpenStack client:

```
openstack --version
```

You should see a version number output, confirming that the client is installed.

- Source the OpenStack RC File

To use the Glance CLI, you need to source your OpenStack RC file, which contains environment variables that define how the CLI interacts with your OpenStack environment. Source the RC file using:

```
source ~/openstack.rc
```

Replace **~/openstack.rc** with the path to your RC file. This step ensures that the CLI commands are authenticated and directed to the correct OpenStack environment.

Creating an Image

With the Glance CLI installed and configured, you can now create and register images in Glance.

Obtain or Build an Image

You need an image file that you can upload to Glance. This could be a pre-built image such as an Ubuntu Cloud image or a custom-built image that you've prepared. For this example, we'll use a CirrOS image, which is a minimal cloud image often used for testing.

```
wget http://download.cirros-cloud.net/0.5.2/cirros-0.5.2-
x86_64-disk.img
```

Create an Image in Glance

Use the Glance CLI to create an image entry in Glance. This command registers the image without uploading the data:

```
openstack image create "CirrOS" --disk-format qcow2 --
container-format bare --file cirros-0.5.2-x86_64-disk.img
--public
```

Here,

- **"CirrOS"**: The name of the image.
- **--disk-format qcow2**: The format of the image file.
- **--container-format bare**: Specifies that the image is not within another container format.
- **--file cirros-0.5.2-x86_64-disk.img**: The path to the image file.
- **--public**: Makes the image public so that any project in the OpenStack environment can use it.

Verify Image Creation

After the image is created, verify that it is available in Glance:

```
openstack image list
```

This command should display the CirrOS image along with its ID, status, and other details.

Registering Image in Glance

In some cases, you might have an image stored in a different location or need to re-register an existing image. The registration process is similar to the creation process but focuses on associating metadata with an existing image.

Registering an External Image

If you have an image stored externally (for example, in an HTTP repository or object storage), you can register it without uploading it directly:

```
openstack image create "External Image" --disk-format
qcow2 --container-format bare --location
http://example.com/images/external-image.qcow2 --public
```

Here, **--location** specifies the URL where the image is stored. Glance will reference this URL when the image is needed.

Updating Image Metadata

If you need to update the metadata of an existing image (such as its visibility or format), you can do so using the following command:

```
openstack image set --property key=value --public
<image_id>
```

Replace **<image_id>** with the ID of the image you want to update. This command allows you to modify the properties and access control of the image.

Deleting an Image

If you need to remove an image from Glance, you can do so easily with the following command:

```
openstack image delete <image_id>
```

This command will remove the image from the Glance repository.

With these above skills, you can ensure that the necessary virtual machine templates are readily available for deployment across their OpenStack environment. Do not forget that proper image management is the foundation for efficient cloud operations, enabling rapid and consistent instance creation.

Recipe 2: Building Custom Images with Cloud-Init

Cloud-Init is a widely used tool for initializing cloud instances. It is responsible for performing the initial configuration of a cloud instance when it first boots, such as setting up SSH keys, configuring the hostname, installing packages, and running user-defined scripts. Cloud-Init is supported by most Linux distributions and cloud platforms, including OpenStack, making it an essential tool for customizing and automating instance deployments.

By integrating Cloud-Init with OpenStack's Glance service, you can create custom images that automatically configure themselves based on your requirements, allowing for seamless, hands-off deployments. In this recipe, we will first learn how to get started with Cloud-Init, and then we will demonstrate how to build and register custom images in Glance using Cloud-Init.

Getting Started with Cloud-Init

Installing Cloud-Init

Most modern Linux distributions come with Cloud-Init pre-installed. However, if you are working with a base image that doesn't include Cloud-Init, you can install it manually. For example, on an Ubuntu system, you would run:

```
sudo apt update

sudo apt install -y cloud-init
```

On a CentOS or RHEL system, use:

```
sudo yum install -y cloud-init
```

Once installed, Cloud-Init automatically runs on the first boot of the instance, performing the initial configuration based on metadata provided by the cloud platform.

Understanding Cloud-Init Configuration

Cloud-Init uses several data sources to configure the instance, such as user-data and meta-data files. These files are typically provided by the cloud platform (in this case, OpenStack) and contain configuration instructions.

- **User-Data**: This is where you define the custom scripts and configuration that you want to be applied to the instance. For example, you can use user-data to install packages, create files, or run custom commands.

- **Meta-Data**: This provides instance-specific information, such as the instance ID, hostname, and SSH public keys.

These configurations are typically written in YAML format and are passed to the instance at boot time.

Sample Cloud-Init Configuration

Here is a basic example of a Cloud-Init configuration that updates the package list and installs Apache:

```
#cloud-config

package_update: true

packages:

  - apache2

runcmd:

  - echo "Hello, World!" > /var/www/html/index.html
```

This configuration tells Cloud-Init to update the package list, install Apache, and create a simple web page.

Building a Custom Image with Cloud-Init

Now that we understand the basics of Cloud-Init, let's build a custom image that includes Cloud-Init and is pre-configured with our desired settings.

Prepare a Base Image

Start with a base image that you want to customize. You can use an existing Ubuntu or CentOS image, or create your own from scratch. For this example, we'll use an Ubuntu image.

If you don't have a base image, you can download one:

```
wget http://cloud-images.ubuntu.com/focal/current/focal-
server-cloudimg-amd64.img
```

Customize the Image with Cloud-Init

Use a tool like **virt-customize** from the libguestfs suite to inject files into the image. First, install libguestfs-tools if you don't already have it:

```
sudo apt install -y libguestfs-tools
```

Then, inject your Cloud-Init configuration into the image:

```
sudo virt-customize -a focal-server-cloudimg-amd64.img --
run-command 'cloud-init clean'
```

```
sudo virt-customize -a focal-server-cloudimg-amd64.img --
copy-in cloud-init-config.yaml:/etc/cloud/cloud.cfg.d/
```

Here, **cloud-init-config.yaml** is your custom Cloud-Init configuration file, which is copied into the **/etc/cloud/cloud.cfg.d/** directory within the image.

Verify the Cloud-Init Configuration

After injecting the configuration, you can verify it by mounting the image and inspecting the files:

```
sudo guestmount -a focal-server-cloudimg-amd64.img -i
/mnt

cat /mnt/etc/cloud/cloud.cfg.d/cloud-init-config.yaml

sudo guestunmount /mnt
```

This step ensures that the configuration has been correctly applied to the image.

Upload the Custom Image to Glance

Once your custom image is ready, the next step is to upload it to Glance so that it can be used to launch instances in OpenStack.

```
openstack image create "Custom-Ubuntu-CloudInit" --file
focal-server-cloudimg-amd64.img --disk-format qcow2 --
container-format bare --public
```

This command uploads the customized image to Glance and makes it available for use in the OpenStack environment.

Launch an Instance using Custom Image

Finally, launch a new instance using the custom image to see Cloud-Init in action:

```
openstack server create --flavor m1.small --image Custom-
Ubuntu-CloudInit --network private --key-name mykey
custom-instance
```

Once the instance is launched, SSH into it and verify that the Cloud-Init configuration has been applied:

```
ssh -i mykey.pem ubuntu@<instance_ip>
```

Check if Apache is installed and running:

```
systemctl status apache2
```

You should also see the "Hello, World!" message on the default web page. Now, to streamline the process of building and uploading custom images with Cloud-Init, you can automate it using a script.

Here's an example of a bash script that automates the steps above:

```
#!/bin/bash


# Variables

IMAGE_NAME="Custom-Ubuntu-CloudInit"

BASE_IMAGE="focal-server-cloudimg-amd64.img"

CLOUD_INIT_CONFIG="cloud-init-config.yaml"


# Download the base image
wget http://cloud-
images.ubuntu.com/focal/current/$BASE_IMAGE


# Install libguestfs-tools if not already installed

sudo apt install -y libguestfs-tools
```

```
# Inject Cloud-Init config into the image

sudo virt-customize -a $BASE_IMAGE --run-command 'cloud-
init clean'

sudo virt-customize -a $BASE_IMAGE --copy-in
$CLOUD_INIT_CONFIG:/etc/cloud/cloud.cfg.d/


# Upload the image to Glance

openstack image create "$IMAGE_NAME" --file $BASE_IMAGE -
-disk-format qcow2 --container-format bare --public


# Launch an instance from the custom image (optional)

# openstack server create --flavor m1.small --image
$IMAGE_NAME --network private --key-name mykey custom-
instance
```

This above script automates the process of downloading the base image, customizing it with Cloud-Init, and uploading it to Glance. Overall in this recipe, we learned how to get started with Cloud-Init and how to build custom images using it in Glance.

Recipe 3: Managing Image Metadata and Properties

Introduction to Image Metadata and Properties

Glance plays a critical role in managing images that serve as templates for launching virtual machines. These images are not just raw data files; they come with associated metadata and properties that describe various aspects of the image, such as its format, architecture, size, and specific configurations. Properly managing image metadata optimizes image retrieval, organizing images efficiently, and ensures that the right images are selected during instance creation.

This recipe will explore the various tasks associated with managing image metadata and properties in Glance. We'll cover how to view, add, update, and delete metadata properties for images, as well as how to use these properties to enhance image management in your OpenStack environment.

Understanding Image Metadata and Properties

What Are Metadata and Properties?

- **Metadata**: Metadata refers to a set of data that describes and gives information about other data—in this case, the image. Metadata can include information such as the image name, size, checksum, disk format, and more.

- **Properties**: Properties are specific attributes associated with an image, which can be custom-defined to suit specific use cases. These properties might include details such as operating system type, architecture, image version, and custom tags.

Why Manage Metadata and Properties?

Managing image metadata and properties allows you to:

- **Organize and Categorize**: By assigning meaningful properties to images, you can easily organize and categorize them based on their purpose or configuration.

- **Optimize Image Selection**: Properties enable more precise image selection when launching instances, ensuring that the most appropriate image is used.

- **Enhance Searchability**: With well-managed metadata, you can quickly search and retrieve images that match specific criteria.

- **Implement Policies**: Properties can be used to enforce policies, such as ensuring that only images with certain security configurations are deployed in production environments.

Viewing Image Metadata and Properties

Before managing image properties, it's important to understand how to view the existing metadata and properties associated with an image.

- List All Images with Basic Metadata

Use the following command to list all images in Glance along with their basic metadata:

```
openstack image list
```

This command displays a table with columns such as ID, Name, Status, and Visibility. While this provides a quick overview, it doesn't show detailed properties.

- View Detailed Metadata and Properties of a Specific Image

To view detailed metadata and properties of a specific image, use the **openstack image show** command followed by the image ID or name:

```
openstack image show <image_id>
```

This command provides a comprehensive list of metadata and properties, including the disk format, container format, size, checksum, and any custom properties.

Adding and Updating Image Metadata Properties

After viewing the metadata, you might want to add new properties or update existing ones to better manage your images.

Add Custom Properties to an Image

Custom properties can be added to an image to provide additional information that is not covered by the default metadata. For example, you might want to tag an image with the operating system version or designate it as a "golden" image.

To add a custom property, use the **openstack image set** command:

```
openstack image set --property <key>=<value>
<image_id_or_name>
```

Example:

```
openstack image set --property os_version="Ubuntu 20.04"
--property image_type="golden" cirros
```

In this example, two properties are added to the image named **cirros**:

- **os_version** is set to "Ubuntu 20.04".
- **image_type** is set to "golden".

Update Existing Properties

If you need to update an existing property, use the same **openstack image set** command with the new value for the property:

```
openstack image set --property os_version="Ubuntu 22.04"
<image_id_or_name>
```

This command updates the **os_version** property of the specified image to "Ubuntu 22.04".

Verify Added or Updated Properties

After adding or updating properties, it's important to verify that the changes have been applied correctly:

```
openstack image show <image_id_or_name>
```

This command will display the updated list of properties, including any new or modified ones.

Deleting Image Properties

In some cases, you might need to remove a property from an image, especially if it's no longer relevant or was added by mistake.

Delete a Specific Property

To delete a specific property from an image, use the **--property** flag with the **openstack image unset** command:

```
openstack image unset --property <key> <image_id_or_name>
```

Example:

```
openstack image unset --property image_type cirros
```

This command removes the **image_type** property from the **cirros** image.

Verify Property Deletion

After deleting a property, verify that it has been removed by using the **openstack image show** command:

```
openstack image show <image_id_or_name>
```

The output should no longer include the deleted property.

Using Image Metadata for Enhanced Management

Image metadata can be leveraged to enhance image management, particularly in large-scale OpenStack environments where many images are in use.

Organizing Images by Tags

Tags are a powerful way to categorize images. You can add tags to images using the **openstack image set** command:

```
openstack image set --tag <tag_name> <image_id_or_name>
```

Example:

```
openstack image set --tag "production" cirros
```

This command tags the **cirros** image with "production".

Searching for Tagged Images

You can search for images by tags, making it easy to retrieve all images that belong to a specific category:

```
openstack image list --tag <tag_name>
```

Example:

```
openstack image list --tag "production"
```

This command lists all images tagged with "production".

Implementing Image Policies Based on Properties

You can enforce policies based on image properties. For example, you might want to restrict certain operations (like launching instances) to images that meet specific criteria. Now, when launching an instance, you can filter images based on properties:

```
openstack server create --image <image_id_or_name> --flavor <flavor> --network <network> <server_name>
```

Ensure that the image selected matches the properties you've defined (e.g., only using images tagged with **golden** or **production**).

Automating Metadata Management

For environments with many images, automating the management of image metadata and properties can save significant time and reduce errors.

Using Scripts to Automate Metadata Tasks

Bash scripts can be used to automate the addition, updating, or removal of image properties. Here's a simple script to tag all images of a specific operating system:

```bash
#!/bin/bash

OS_VERSION="Ubuntu 20.04"

TAG="ubuntu-20.04"



images=$(openstack image list --property
os_version=$OS_VERSION -f value -c ID)



for image in $images; do

    openstack image set --tag $TAG $image

done
```

This script tags all images with the **os_version** property set to "Ubuntu 20.04" with the tag "ubuntu-20.04".

Automated Reporting on Image Metadata

Generate reports on image metadata to monitor and review the properties of all images in your environment. Here's a simple example of how you might generate a report:

```bash
openstack image list -f json > images.json
```

```
jq '.[] | {ID: .ID, Name: .Name, Properties:
.Properties}' images.json > image_report.json
```

This script generates a JSON report of all images and their properties, making it easier to review and manage image metadata.

Best Practices for Managing Image Metadata and Properties

To ensure efficient and effective management of image metadata and properties, consider the following best practices:

- Standardize Property Names

Use standardized names for properties to ensure consistency across all images. For example, always use **os_version** to describe the operating system version.

- Document Metadata Standards

Maintain documentation that defines the metadata and properties used in your environment. This documentation should describe the purpose of each property and how it should be used.

- Regularly Review and Update Properties

Periodically review image properties to ensure they are still relevant and accurate. Remove outdated or unnecessary properties to keep the metadata clean and useful.

- Automate Where Possible

Use scripts and automation tools to manage image properties, especially in large environments where manual management is time-consuming and prone to errors.

- Leverage Properties for Policy Enforcement

Use image properties to enforce operational policies, such as restricting which images can be used in production environments or automating compliance checks based on metadata.

By effectively managing metadata, you can optimize the organization, retrieval, and use of images within your OpenStack environment. Whether it's tagging images for easy categorization or using properties to enforce policies, managing metadata is key to maintaining a well-organized and efficient cloud infrastructure. Also, through the use of automation and best practices, you can ensure that image management remains scalable, consistent, and aligned with operational goals.

Recipe 4: Configuring Glance to Use Different Backends (Swift, Ceph)

Introduction to Object Storage Systems

When managing images in OpenStack, the choice of storage backend for Glance is vital for performance, scalability, and reliability. Glance supports various storage backends, with OpenStack Swift and Ceph being two of the most popular options. Each backend offers unique advantages, making them suitable for different use cases.

Swift Object Storage

OpenStack Swift is an object storage system designed to store and retrieve large amounts of unstructured data at scale. Swift is particularly well-suited for cloud environments that require high availability and fault tolerance. It achieves this by distributing data across multiple nodes and replicating it to ensure durability. Swift's architecture is designed for scalability, making it an excellent choice for environments that expect significant growth in storage needs.

Ceph Object Storage

Ceph is a distributed storage system that provides object, block, and file storage in a unified platform. Unlike Swift, which focuses solely on object storage, Ceph offers a more versatile solution with its ability to handle different types of data. Ceph is highly regarded for its performance, scalability, and resilience, making it ideal for environments that require a high level of data redundancy and performance, especially when dealing with block storage for virtual machines and object storage for large datasets.

Choosing the Right Storage System

Given GitforGits' requirements, Ceph is likely the better choice for a few key reasons:

1. **Unified Storage**: Ceph provides a unified storage solution that can handle both object and block storage. This is particularly useful for GitforGits, which may benefit from using Ceph not only for Glance but also for Cinder (block storage) and Nova (ephemeral storage).

2. **Scalability and Performance**: Ceph is designed to scale out with ease, allowing GitforGits to expand its storage capacity as needed without significant reconfiguration. Additionally, Ceph's architecture ensures high performance, which is essential for quick image retrieval and instance boot times.

3. **Data Redundancy and Resilience**: Ceph's ability to replicate data across multiple nodes ensures that GitforGits' images are protected against hardware failures, making it a reliable choice for mission-critical applications.

Given these advantages, we will proceed with configuring Glance to use Ceph as its backend storage system for GitforGits.

Configuring Glance to use Ceph

Now that we've decided to use Ceph as the backend storage for Glance, we'll walk through the steps to configure Glance accordingly.

Prepare the Ceph Cluster

Before configuring Glance, ensure that the Ceph cluster is properly set up and running. If Ceph is not yet installed, you'll need to install and configure it first. For this recipe, we assume that Ceph is already installed and functional.

Create a Ceph Pool for Glance

Glance requires a dedicated pool in Ceph where images will be stored. Create a new pool named **images**:

```
ceph osd pool create images 128 128
```

The command above creates a pool named **images** with 128 placement groups. You can adjust the number of placement groups based on your cluster size and requirements.

Create a Client Keyring

Glance needs access to the Ceph cluster via a client keyring. Create a client key for Glance:

```
ceph auth get-or-create client.glance mon 'allow r' osd
'allow class-read object_prefix rbd_children, allow rwx
pool=images'
```

This command creates a new keyring entry for the **client.glance** user, granting it read and write access to the **images** pool.

Save the keyring to a file:

```
ceph auth get-or-create client.glance >
/etc/ceph/ceph.client.glance.keyring
```

Ensure the keyring file is securely stored and accessible by the Glance service.

Install and Configure Ceph on the Glance Node

Install Ceph Client Packages

On the node where Glance is running, install the necessary Ceph client packages:

```
sudo apt update

sudo apt install -y ceph ceph-common
```

These packages allow Glance to communicate with the Ceph cluster.

Configure Ceph for Glance

Ensure that the Ceph configuration file (**/etc/ceph/ceph.conf**) is present on the Glance node. This file should contain the necessary configuration for connecting to the Ceph cluster. If not already present, copy the **ceph.conf** from a Ceph node:

```
scp user@ceph-node:/etc/ceph/ceph.conf /etc/ceph/
```

Replace **user@ceph-node** with the appropriate user and Ceph node hostname. And then verify that the configuration is correct by listing the Ceph pools:

```
ceph osd lspools
```

You should see the **images** pool listed.

Configure Glance to use Ceph

Now that the Ceph client is configured on the Glance node, it's time to configure Glance to use Ceph as its backend.

- Edit the Glance Configuration File

Open the Glance configuration file (**/etc/glance/glance-api.conf**) and update the **[DEFAULT]** and **[glance_store]** sections to use Ceph.

```
[DEFAULT]

# Other existing configurations...

show_image_direct_url = True
```

```
[glance_store]

stores = rbd,file,http

default_store = rbd

rbd_store_pool = images

rbd_store_user = glance

rbd_store_ceph_conf = /etc/ceph/ceph.conf

rbd_store_chunk_size = 8

rbd_store_image_format = 2
```

- Key configuration options:
  - **stores**: Lists the available storage backends. Here, **rbd** (RADOS Block Device, used by Ceph) is listed.
  - **default_store**: Specifies **rbd** as the default storage backend for Glance.
  - **rbd_store_pool**: Specifies the Ceph pool where images will be stored.
  - **rbd_store_user**: Specifies the Ceph client user (**glance**).
  - **rbd_store_ceph_conf**: Points to the Ceph configuration file.

Ensure that the **glance** user on the Glance node has the appropriate permissions to access the Ceph keyring:

```
sudo chown glance:glance
/etc/ceph/ceph.client.glance.keyring

sudo chmod 600 /etc/ceph/ceph.client.glance.keyring
```

After updating the configuration, restart the Glance API service to apply the changes:

```
sudo systemctl restart glance-api
```

Verify the Configuration

- Upload an Image to Glance

To verify that Glance is correctly using Ceph as the backend, upload a new image:

```
openstack image create "Ceph-Test-Image" --file
/path/to/image.img --disk-format qcow2 --container-format
bare --public
```

Replace **/path/to/image.img** with the path to the image file you want to upload.

- Verify Image Storage in Ceph

Check that the image has been stored in the Ceph pool by listing the objects in the **images** pool:

```
rados -p images ls
```

You should see objects corresponding to the image you uploaded.

- Launch an Instance Using the Ceph-Backed Image

Finally, launch an instance using the image stored in Ceph to confirm that everything is working correctly:

```
openstack server create --flavor m1.small --image Ceph-
Test-Image --network private --key-name mykey ceph-
instance
```

Monitor the instance launch and ensure that the image is being retrieved from Ceph without any issues.

Managing and Monitoring the Ceph Backend

Monitor Ceph Health

Regularly monitor the health of the Ceph cluster to ensure that Glance continues to have reliable access to image data:

```
ceph status
```

This command provides an overview of the Ceph cluster's health, including any warnings or errors.

Expanding Storage

As the image repository grows, you may need to expand the Ceph storage pool. Add more OSDs (Object Storage Daemons) to the Ceph cluster to increase capacity and performance:

```
ceph osd create
```

Follow the Ceph documentation to add and configure new OSDs.

Backup and Recovery

Implement a backup and recovery strategy for your Ceph cluster. Ensure that critical data, such as images, are backed up regularly. Ceph provides snapshot capabilities that can be used to create point-in-time backups of images.

```
rbd snap create images/<image_name>@backup
```

In this recipe, we explored the configuration of Glance to use Ceph as the storage backend for GitforGits. With Ceph as the backend, we can benefit from a robust and scalable storage solution that ensures images are stored securely and can be retrieved quickly for instance deployment.

Recipe 5: Automating Image Uploads with Glance CLI

Introduction to Automating Image Uploads

In dynamic cloud environments, such as the one managed by GitforGits, frequent updates to virtual machine images are common. These updates may include new security patches, application configurations, or entirely new OS versions. Manually uploading and managing these images in Glance can become time-consuming and error-prone. Automating the image upload process using the Glance CLI ensures that images are consistently and efficiently updated, minimizing manual intervention and reducing the risk of errors.

In this recipe, we will learn how to automate the process of uploading images to Glance using the Glance CLI. We will create a script that can be scheduled to run at regular intervals or triggered by specific events, such as the availability of a new image version. This approach will streamline the management of images, ensuring that the latest versions are always available in Glance.

Creating the Automation Script

Before we begin automating the image upload process, ensure that the following prerequisites are met:

The Glance CLI should be installed on the system where the automation script will run. This was covered in a previous recipe.

The OpenStack RC file, which contains environment variables for authentication, must be sourced before running the script. This allows the script to interact with Glance using the correct credentials.

The image files to be uploaded should be accessible from the system where the script will run. These files could be stored locally or fetched from a remote repository.

Now, we'll create a Bash script that automates the image upload process. The script will include the following steps:

- **Source the OpenStack RC File**: This ensures that the script is authenticated with the OpenStack environment.

- **Check for Existing Images**: The script will check if the image already exists in Glance. If it does, the script will decide whether to replace the existing image based on versioning or timestamp criteria.

- **Upload the New Image**: If a new image is available, the script will upload it to Glance.

- **Verify the Upload**: After uploading, the script will verify that the image has been successfully added to Glance.

Following is the sample script of **auto_upload_image.sh**

```bash
#!/bin/bash


# Define variables

IMAGE_NAME="Custom-Ubuntu-CloudInit"

IMAGE_FILE="/path/to/image.img"

DISK_FORMAT="qcow2"

CONTAINER_FORMAT="bare"

IMAGE_VERSION="v1.2"  # Optional versioning


# Source the OpenStack RC file
```

```
source ~/openstack.rc


# Check if the image already exists

existing_image=$(openstack image list --name $IMAGE_NAME
-f value -c ID)


if [ -n "$existing_image" ]; then

    echo "Image '$IMAGE_NAME' already exists with ID:
$existing_image"


    # Check if the existing image should be replaced
(e.g., based on version or other criteria)

    existing_version=$(openstack image show
$existing_image -f value -c properties | grep "version")


    if [ "$existing_version" == "$IMAGE_VERSION" ]; then

        echo "The existing image is already at version
$IMAGE_VERSION. No need to upload."

        exit 0

    else

        echo "Updating the image to version
$IMAGE_VERSION..."

        openstack image delete $existing_image
```

```
    fi
fi


# Upload the new image

echo "Uploading new image '$IMAGE_NAME'..."

openstack image create "$IMAGE_NAME" \

    --file $IMAGE_FILE \

    --disk-format $DISK_FORMAT \

    --container-format $CONTAINER_FORMAT \

    --property version="$IMAGE_VERSION" \

    --public


# Verify the upload

uploaded_image=$(openstack image list --name $IMAGE_NAME
-f value -c ID)


if [ -n "$uploaded_image" ]; then

    echo "Image '$IMAGE_NAME' successfully uploaded with
ID: $uploaded_image"

else

    echo "Image upload failed."

    exit 1
```

```
fi
```

In the above script:

- **IMAGE_NAME** specifies the name of the image to be uploaded.

- **IMAGE_FILE** points to the location of the image file.

- **DISK_FORMAT** and **CONTAINER_FORMAT** define the format of the image.

- **IMAGE_VERSION** is an optional variable that can be used to track the version of the image.

The **source ~/openstack.rc** command ensures that the script has the necessary environment variables to interact with OpenStack. The script uses **openstack image list** to check if an image with the specified name already exists.

If the image exists, the script checks if the version matches the version defined in the script. If the versions match, the script exits without uploading a new image. Otherwise, the existing image is deleted to make way for the new version.

The script uses **openstack image create** to upload the image. It sets the image name, file path, disk format, container format, and any additional properties such as version. The **--public** flag makes the image available to all projects. This can be adjusted based on your access requirements.

After uploading, the script verifies that the image was successfully added to Glance by checking the image list again.

Scheduling the Script with Cron

To fully automate the image upload process, you can schedule the script to run at regular intervals using cron. For example, you might want to check for new image versions daily and upload them if available.

- Edit the Crontab

Open the crontab for the current user:

```
crontab -e
```

- Add a Cron Job

Add a new cron job to run the script every day at 2 AM:

```
0 2 * * * /path/to/auto_upload_image.sh >>
/var/log/auto_upload_image.log 2>&1
```

This line schedules the script to run daily at 2 AM and logs the output to **/var/log/auto_upload_image.log**.

The above script can be extended to handle more complex scenarios:

Multiple Image Uploads

If you need to upload multiple images, you can extend the script to loop through a list of images:

```
declare -A IMAGES=(

    ["Ubuntu-20.04"]="/path/to/ubuntu-20.04.img"

    ["CentOS-8"]="/path/to/centos-8.img"

)

for IMAGE_NAME in "${!IMAGES[@]}"; do

    IMAGE_FILE="${IMAGES[$IMAGE_NAME]}"

    # Repeat the upload process for each image

    # ...

done
```

This allows you to manage and automate the upload of multiple images in a single script.

Custom Metadata and Tags

You can add custom metadata and tags during the image upload process by extending the **openstack image create** command with additional **--property** and **--tag** options:

```
openstack image create "$IMAGE_NAME" \

    --file $IMAGE_FILE \
```

```
    --disk-format $DISK_FORMAT \

    --container-format $CONTAINER_FORMAT \

    --property version="$IMAGE_VERSION" \

    --property os_version="Ubuntu 20.04" \

    --tag "production" \

    --public
```

Fetching Images from Remote Sources

If your images are stored in a remote repository, you can extend the script to fetch the latest image before uploading it:

```
wget -N http://repository.example.com/images/latest.img -
O /path/to/image.img
```

The **-N** option ensures that the image is only downloaded if it's newer than the local copy. You can also configure the script to send notifications or alerts if an image upload fails. For example, you can use **mail** or **sendmail** to send an email if the script encounters an error:

```
if [ -z "$uploaded_image" ]; then

    echo "Image upload failed." | mail -s "Image Upload
Failure" admin@example.com

    exit 1

fi
```

Testing and Monitoring

Before scheduling the script with cron, manually test it to ensure it works as expected:

```
./auto_upload_image.sh
```

Verify that the image is uploaded correctly and that the script handles existing images as intended. After scheduling the script with cron, regularly monitor the logs to ensure that the uploads are successful and to troubleshoot any issues that arise:

```
tail -f /var/log/auto_upload_image.log
```

This command will display the log output in real-time, helping you keep track of the script's execution.

Recipe 6: Managing Image Versions and Updates

Introduction to Image Versioning and Updates

In any cloud environment, managing different versions of virtual machine images is critical to maintaining consistency, security, and stability. As updates to operating systems, applications, and configurations are released, it's essential to ensure that your cloud infrastructure is running the correct version of each image. This recipe focuses on managing image versions and updates within OpenStack's Glance service, allowing you to efficiently track, update, and maintain image versions across your environment.

Image versioning in Glance involves creating, tagging, and maintaining multiple versions of images to ensure that you can deploy the correct image for each scenario. This process includes updating existing images, rolling back to previous versions when necessary, and deprecating older versions as they become obsolete. By implementing a structured versioning strategy, GitforGits can ensure that all instances are based on the latest, most secure, and stable image versions.

Creating and Tagging Image Versions

The first step in managing image versions is to establish a versioning strategy that aligns with your organization's needs. This strategy could involve using semantic versioning (e.g., 1.0, 1.1, 2.0) or another system that suits your workflow.

Creating a New Image Version

When you create a new version of an image, it's important to tag it with a version number to distinguish it from previous versions. For example, if you have an image named **Ubuntu-20.04** and you want to create a new version **1.1**, you would do the following:

```
openstack image create "Ubuntu-20.04-v1.1" \
```

```
--file /path/to/ubuntu-20.04-v1.1.img \

--disk-format qcow2 \

--container-format bare \

--property version="1.1" \

--property os_version="Ubuntu 20.04" \

--public
```

This command uploads the new image version and tags it with the **version** property, making it easy to identify.

Tagging Images

Tags are another way to manage image versions. For example, you can tag an image as **latest** to indicate that it is the most current version:

```
openstack image set --tag latest Ubuntu-20.04-v1.1
```

If you later upload a new version, you can remove the **latest** tag from the old version and apply it to the new one:

```
openstack image unset --tag latest Ubuntu-20.04-v1.1

openstack image set --tag latest Ubuntu-20.04-v1.2
```

This method allows you to quickly identify and deploy the latest image version.

Viewing Image Versions

To view all versions of a particular image, you can use the following command:

```
openstack image list --property os_version="Ubuntu 20.04"
```

This command lists all images with the specified operating system version, allowing you to see the available versions.

Updating Images

Updating images in Glance involves replacing older versions with newer ones, ensuring that all instances are using the latest updates. This is particularly important for applying security patches or configuration changes.

Uploading an Updated Image

When a new version of an image becomes available, upload it to Glance with an incremented version number:

```
openstack image create "Ubuntu-20.04-v1.2" \

    --file /path/to/ubuntu-20.04-v1.2.img \

    --disk-format qcow2 \

    --container-format bare \

    --property version="1.2" \

    --property os_version="Ubuntu 20.04" \

    --public
```

This command uploads the updated image and tags it with the new version number.

Deprecating Older Versions

To encourage users to move to the newer image, you can deprecate the older versions by setting a custom property or removing the **public** visibility:

```
openstack image set --property deprecated=true Ubuntu-
20.04-v1.0
```

Alternatively, you can make the older image private, so it's no longer visible to all users:

```
openstack image set --private Ubuntu-20.04-v1.0
```

Deprecating older versions helps to ensure that new instances are launched with the latest image.

Replacing Instances with Updated Images

Once a new image version is available, you may need to update existing instances. While OpenStack does not allow direct in-place image upgrades, you can create a new instance from the updated image and then migrate data from the old instance.

Following are the example steps:

- Launch a New Instance

Create a new instance using the updated image:

```
openstack server create --flavor m1.small --image Ubuntu-
20.04-v1.2 --network private --key-name mykey updated-
instance
```

- Migrate Data

Use tools like **rsync** or **scp** to migrate data from the old instance to the new one.

- Update DNS or Load Balancers

If the instance is part of a load-balanced application, update the DNS records or load balancer configuration to point to the new instance.

- Delete the Old Instance

Once the migration is complete, delete the old instance:

```
openstack server delete old-instance
```

This process ensures that your applications are always running on the latest, most secure image versions.

Rolling Back to Previous Versions

Sometimes, after deploying a new image version, you may discover issues that require rolling back to a previous version. Glance's versioning capabilities make this process straightforward.

- Identifying the Previous Version

List the available versions of an image to identify the version to which you need to roll back:

```
openstack image list --property os_version="Ubuntu 20.04"
```

Find the version number or image name you wish to revert to.

- Launching an Instance from a Previous Version

Use the previous image version to launch a new instance:

```
openstack server create --flavor m1.small --image Ubuntu-
20.04-v1.0 --network private --key-name mykey rollback-
instance
```

This command launches an instance from the selected previous version.

- Updating or Reverting Tags

If you use tags to manage versions, revert the **latest** tag to the previous version to ensure that new instances are launched with the rollback image:

```
openstack image unset --tag latest Ubuntu-20.04-v1.2

openstack image set --tag latest Ubuntu-20.04-v1.0
```

- Communicating the Rollback

Ensure that any rollback is communicated to the relevant teams and users. You may also want to mark the problematic version as deprecated or remove it entirely to prevent further issues:

```
openstack image delete Ubuntu-20.04-v1.2
```

Alternatively, keep it private for further testing:

```
openstack image set --private Ubuntu-20.04-v1.2
```

Automating Image Version Management

To streamline image version management, consider automating the process using scripts and cron jobs.

Automated Image Upload Script

You can automate the image upload process with a script that checks for new versions and uploads them to Glance:

```bash
#!/bin/bash

IMAGE_NAME="Ubuntu-20.04"

NEW_VERSION="v1.3"

IMAGE_FILE="/path/to/ubuntu-20.04-v1.3.img"


existing_image=$(openstack image list --name $IMAGE_NAME-$NEW_VERSION -f value -c ID)


if [ -z "$existing_image" ]; then

    echo "Uploading new image version $NEW_VERSION..."

    openstack image create "$IMAGE_NAME-$NEW_VERSION" \

        --file $IMAGE_FILE \

        --disk-format qcow2 \

        --container-format bare \

        --property version="$NEW_VERSION" \

        --property os_version="Ubuntu 20.04" \

        --public

else

    echo "Image version $NEW_VERSION already exists."

fi
```

This script checks if a specific image version exists and uploads it if it does not.

Automating Version Tagging

Extend the script to manage tags, ensuring that the latest image version is always tagged correctly:

```
# Remove the latest tag from the old version

openstack image unset --tag latest Ubuntu-20.04-v1.2


# Set the latest tag on the new version

openstack image set --tag latest Ubuntu-20.04-v1.3
```

Then, schedule the script to run automatically, checking for and uploading new image versions:

```
crontab -e
```

Add a cron job to check for new versions every day at 2 AM:

```
0 2 * * * /path/to/upload_image_version.sh >>
/var/log/upload_image_version.log 2>&1
```

This ensures that new image versions are consistently uploaded and managed without manual intervention.

Best Practices for Managing Image Versions

To effectively manage image versions and updates, consider the following best practices:

- Standardize Versioning

Use a consistent versioning scheme (e.g., semantic versioning) across all images to simplify management and reduce confusion.

- Document Versioning and Updates

Maintain clear documentation that tracks the version history of each image, including changes, updates, and the rationale for deprecating or rolling back versions.

- Test Before Deployment

Always test new image versions in a staging environment before deploying them to production. This helps catch issues early and minimizes the risk of downtime or data loss.

- Use Tags for Quick Identification

Leverage tags like **latest**, **stable**, or **deprecated** to quickly identify and manage image versions, making it easier for users to select the correct image.

- Automate Where Possible

Automate the process of uploading, tagging, and managing image versions to reduce the potential for human error and ensure consistency across the environment.

- Monitor and Audit Image Usage

Regularly monitor which image versions are in use and audit them to ensure compliance with security policies and operational requirements.

In the above, we covered creating and tagging new image versions, updating images, rolling back to previous versions when necessary, and automating the management process. By implementing a structured approach to image versioning, GitforGits can ensure that its cloud environment remains consistent, secure, and up-to-date, with minimal manual intervention.

Recipe 7: Securing and Encrypting Images in Glance

In cloud environments, images are one of the most critical assets, as they contain the operating systems, applications, and configurations necessary to run virtual machines. However, these images can also be a significant security vulnerability if not properly protected. Unauthorized access to images can lead to data breaches, system compromise, and the introduction of malicious software. Recent security research and incidents have highlighted the growing threat landscape, emphasizing the importance of securing and encrypting images stored in cloud environments.

Recent Insights on Image Vulnerabilities

- **Data Breaches**: In several high-profile data breaches, attackers have gained access to unencrypted images, allowing them to extract sensitive information, such as passwords, private keys, and configuration files. This risk is exacerbated in environments where images are publicly accessible or insufficiently protected.

- **Malware Injection**: Attackers may attempt to inject malware or backdoors into images stored in the cloud, which are then unknowingly deployed across multiple instances. This can lead to widespread system compromise and data exfiltration.

- **Lack of Encryption**: A significant number of cloud environments still store images in plaintext, making them vulnerable to interception and unauthorized access, particularly in multi-tenant environments where images are shared across different users and projects.

- **Insider Threats**: Internal actors with access to the cloud infrastructure may misuse their privileges to access, modify, or delete images, leading to potential disruptions or security breaches.

Given these vulnerabilities, it is essential to implement robust security measures for image management in OpenStack's Glance service, and hence this recipe will demonstrate how to secure and encrypt images to mitigate these risks.

Enforcing Secure Access Controls

The first step in securing images is to enforce strict access controls within Glance to limit who can view, modify, or delete images.

- Restricting Image Visibility

By default, images in Glance can be marked as public, private, or shared. To limit access to only authorized users or projects, images should be set to private or shared with specific projects only:

```
openstack image set --private <image_id>
```

This command ensures that only the project that owns the image can view or use it.

- Assigning Image Roles

Implement RBAC to further restrict who can manage images. Assign specific roles that allow only certain users to upload, modify, or delete images:

```
openstack role add --user <user_name> --project <project_name> image-admin
```

This role could be limited to administrators or trusted users, ensuring that image management is tightly controlled.

- Audit and Monitoring

Enable auditing and monitoring of image-related activities. Configure Glance to log all actions performed on images, including creation, deletion, and access attempts:

```
sudo nano /etc/glance/glance-api.conf
```

Enable the following settings:

```
[DEFAULT]
```

```
debug = True


[oslo_middleware]

audit = True

audit_map_file = /etc/glance/api_audit_map.conf
```

After making these changes, restart the Glance API service:

```
sudo systemctl restart glance-api
```

Regularly review these logs for suspicious activities or unauthorized access attempts.

Encrypting Images

Encryption is a critical component of securing images in the cloud. Encrypting images ensures that even if an unauthorized party gains access to the image files, they cannot read or tamper with the contents without the decryption key.

- Encrypting Images at Rest with Ceph

If Glance is configured to use Ceph as the backend, you can leverage Ceph's native encryption capabilities to encrypt images at rest.

- Enable RBD Encryption in Ceph

Ensure that Ceph is configured to support encryption. You can enable encryption on a per-pool basis or for specific images:

```
rbd create --size <size> --image-feature
layering,encryption --image <image_name>
```

This command creates a new encrypted RBD image.

- Upload Encrypted Image to Glance

Once you have an encrypted image, upload it to Glance:

```
openstack image create "Encrypted-Image" --file
/path/to/encrypted_image.img --disk-format qcow2 --
container-format bare --public
```

The image remains encrypted while stored in Ceph, ensuring that it is protected even if an attacker gains access to the storage backend.

- Encrypting Images During Upload

You can also encrypt images before uploading them to Glance, ensuring that they remain secure even during transfer.

- Encrypt the Image File

Use a tool like OpenSSL to encrypt the image file before uploading it:

```
openssl enc -aes-256-cbc -salt -in /path/to/image.img -
out /path/to/encrypted_image.img -k <password>
```

This command encrypts the image using AES-256 encryption.

- Upload the Encrypted Image

Upload the encrypted image to Glance:

```
openstack image create "Encrypted-Image" --file
/path/to/encrypted_image.img --disk-format qcow2 --
container-format bare --public
```

The image is stored in its encrypted form, and the decryption key is required to use it.

- Decrypting the Image for Use

When you need to use the encrypted image, download it from Glance and decrypt it using OpenSSL:

```
openssl enc -aes-256-cbc -d -in
/path/to/encrypted_image.img -out
/path/to/decrypted_image.img -k <password>
```

This command decrypts the image, making it ready for deployment.

- Using Barbican for Key Management

OpenStack Barbican is a service designed for secure storage, provisioning, and management of secrets, such as encryption keys and passwords. Integrating Barbican with Glance allows for automated and secure key management for image encryption.

- Install and Configure Barbican

Ensure Barbican is installed and configured in your OpenStack environment:

```
sudo apt install barbican-api barbican-keystone-listener barbican-worker
```

Configure Barbican to work with Glance by updating the Glance configuration file (**/etc/glance/glance-api.conf**):

```
[barbican]

auth_endpoint = http://<barbican_endpoint>:9311
```

Replace **<barbican_endpoint>** with the actual Barbican service endpoint.

- Create a Secret in Barbican

Create an encryption key in Barbican:

```
openstack secret store --name "glance-image-key" --payload-content-type "application/octet-stream" --payload-content-encoding "base64" --payload <base64-encoded-key>
```

This command stores the encryption key in Barbican, where it can be securely managed.

- Encrypt and Upload the Image Using Barbican

Use the stored key to encrypt the image and upload it to Glance:

```
openstack image create "Barbican-Encrypted-Image" --file /path/to/image.img --disk-format qcow2 --container-format bare --property "encryption-key"="<key_id>" --public
```

Replace **<key_id>** with the ID of the encryption key stored in Barbican.

- Accessing the Encrypted Image

When launching an instance from the encrypted image, Glance automatically retrieves the key from Barbican, ensuring that the image is decrypted and ready for use.

Secure Image Distribution

In addition to encrypting images at rest and during upload, it's important to secure the distribution of images across the network, particularly in multi-tenant environments or when images are shared between different regions.

- Secure Image Transfer Using SSL/TLS

Ensure that all communications between Glance and other OpenStack services, such as Nova and Cinder, are encrypted using SSL/TLS. This prevents unauthorized interception or tampering with image data during transfer.

- Enable SSL/TLS in Glance

Edit the Glance configuration file (**/etc/glance/glance-api.conf**) to enable SSL/TLS:

```
[DEFAULT]

use_ssl = True

cert_file = /etc/ssl/certs/glance.crt

key_file = /etc/ssl/private/glance.key
```

Restart the Glance service to apply the changes:

```
sudo systemctl restart glance-api
```

- Configure Clients to Use SSL/TLS

Ensure that all clients and services interacting with Glance are configured to use SSL/TLS, specifying the appropriate certificate files.

- Implementing Secure Image Replication

In multi-region or multi-cloud environments, where images may need to be replicated across different locations, ensure that image replication is performed securely:

- Use Encrypted Channels for Replication

When replicating images between Glance services in different regions, use encrypted channels (e.g., VPNs or dedicated secure links) to protect the data during transfer.

- Authenticate Replication Endpoints

Ensure that replication endpoints are authenticated, using strong credentials or certificates to prevent unauthorized replication.

Overall in this recipe, we explored the critical aspects of securing and encrypting images in OpenStack's Glance service. Additionally, we covered secure image distribution and the importance of ongoing monitoring and maintenance to ensure the integrity and security of images in your cloud environment.

Summary

To summarize, this chapter focused on mastering image management with Glance, beginning with the process of creating and registering images. We used the Glance CLI to upload and manage images efficiently. We then looked at how to create custom images using Cloud-Init, which allows for automated instance configuration during deployment. The management of image metadata and properties was also covered, with a focus on adding, updating, and utilizing metadata to organize and optimize image usage. We spoke about how to configure Glance to use various storage backends, especially Ceph, to make sure that storing images is fast and scalable.

We also experimented with automating image uploads using the Glance CLI, resulting in efficient and consistent updates to image repositories. We also learned a lot about managing image versions and updates, including how to deal with different versions of images, update existing images, and revert to earlier versions if needed. The chapter concluded by securing and encrypting images, discussing recent vulnerabilities, and demonstrating how to use encryption and secure access controls to protect images in the cloud.

CHAPTER 4: NETWORKING WITH NEUTRON

Introduction

So far in this book, we've covered OpenStack infrastructure setup, Keystone identity management, and Glance image management, all of which provide a solid foundation for creating and managing cloud environments. With Neutron at its heart, this chapter will move our attention to OpenStack's networking capabilities, specifically how to manage connections to internal networks. The recipes in this chapter will provide you with a thorough understanding of configuring and managing OpenStack networking to ensure secure, scalable, and efficient communication across your cloud environment.

We'll start by looking at the various network types supported by Neutron and their specific use cases, so you can choose the best network architecture for your needs. Next, we'll go over how to configure Neutron plugins and agents, which are required for managing various network functions like Layer 2 (L2) and Layer 3 (L3) networking. You will learn how to configure VLAN and VXLAN for L2 networking and how to use L3 routing to manage traffic between networks. In addition, we'll go over how to configure security groups and firewall rules to secure your network, as well as how to manage floating IP addresses and external networks for connectivity.

The chapter will also cover common networking issues and troubleshooting techniques for resolving them efficiently. Finally, we'll look at integrating Neutron with Software-Defined Networking (SDN) controllers, which provide advanced network management capabilities for dynamic and large-scale environments. By the end of this chapter, you will be able to design, implement, and manage robust network architectures for your OpenStack deployment, ensuring reliable and secure connectivity across all cloud infrastructure components.

Recipe 1: Understanding OpenStack Network Types

Introduction to OpenStack Network Types

Neutron is the networking service that provides connectivity as a service between interface devices managed by other OpenStack services. Neutron supports a variety of network types that cater to different use cases and deployment scenarios, enabling flexible and scalable network architectures in cloud environments.

In this recipe, we will explore the different network types that Neutron supports, such as flat, VLAN, VXLAN, and GRE, along with their specific use cases. We'll also consider the existing network topology of GitforGits, our example organization, and ensure that it aligns with Neutron's capabilities. If the current network setup is not fully compatible with Neutron, we will reconfigure it to take advantage of Neutron's features, allowing you to learn and practice effectively.

Exploring Neutron Network Types

Flat Network

A flat network is a simple network type where all instances share a single network, and there is no network segmentation. All instances are on the same broadcast domain. Flat networks are typically used in small-scale environments or for management networks where segregation is not required. Since there is no segmentation, flat networks are not suitable for multi-tenant environments or scenarios where security isolation is critical.

VLAN (Virtual LAN)

VLAN is a network segmentation method that uses the IEEE 802.1Q standard to tag traffic on different virtual networks over a single physical network. Each VLAN has its own unique identifier (VLAN ID). VLANs are ideal for multi-tenant environments where network isolation between tenants is necessary. They provide a secure way to segregate traffic while sharing the same physical infrastructure. VLANs are limited by the number of available VLAN IDs (up to 4096), which can be a constraint in large-scale environments.

VXLAN (Virtual Extensible LAN)

VXLAN is an overlay network technology that extends the VLAN ID space by encapsulating Layer 2 frames within UDP packets, allowing for network segmentation on a much larger scale. VXLAN can support up to 16 million segments. VXLAN is well-suited for large-scale, multi-tenant environments where the limitations of VLAN IDs are a concern. It also allows for more flexible network designs, including crossing physical boundaries. VXLAN requires additional overhead due to encapsulation and may require specific hardware or software support in the network infrastructure.

GRE (Generic Routing Encapsulation)

GRE is another tunneling protocol used to encapsulate network traffic, similar to VXLAN. GRE creates point-to-point links that can tunnel traffic across different networks. GRE is used in scenarios where simple tunneling is required without the need for the additional features provided by VXLAN. It's often used in conjunction with VPNs. GRE lacks the scalability and flexibility of VXLAN and is generally used in more specific, less complex network setups.

GitforGits currently operates a network topology that includes segmented networks for different departments, such as development, testing, and production. The organization requires secure network isolation between these segments while allowing for scalability as the company grows. The network infrastructure uses a mix of VLANs and flat networks, with a focus on simplicity and ease of management.

Given Neutron's capabilities and the needs of GitforGits, the current topology aligns well with a VLAN-based network for segmentation. However, as the company scales, it may be beneficial to transition to VXLAN to accommodate more segments and avoid the limitations of VLAN ID availability.

Configuring Neutron for GitforGits

Given GitforGits' requirements and the existing infrastructure, VLAN is a suitable choice for the current scale. However, to future-proof the network and allow for greater scalability, VXLAN is a more appropriate long-term solution.

To prepare GitforGits for scalability and to take full advantage of Neutron's capabilities, we will transition from VLANs to VXLAN.

- Enable VXLAN in Neutron

Edit the Neutron configuration file (**/etc/neutron/plugins/ml2/ml2_conf.ini**) to enable VXLAN:

```
[ml2]

type_drivers = vxlan

tenant_network_types = vxlan

mechanism_drivers = openvswitch


[ml2_type_vxlan]

vni_ranges = 1000:5000
```

This configuration sets VXLAN as the type driver and defines a range of VXLAN Network Identifiers (VNIs).

- Configure the L2 Agent

Configure the Layer 2 agent (Open vSwitch, in this case) to support VXLAN:

```
sudo nano /etc/neutron/plugins/ml2/openvswitch_agent.ini
```

Ensure the following settings are configured:

```
[ovs]
```

```
local_ip = <compute_node_ip>

tunnel_types = vxlan


[agent]

tunnel_types = vxlan
```

- Restart Neutron Services

After updating the configurations, restart the Neutron services to apply the changes:

```
sudo systemctl restart neutron-server neutron-
openvswitch-agent
```

This ensures that the changes take effect and VXLAN is now the default network type.

- Verifying the Configuration

To verify that the VXLAN configuration is working, create a test network in Neutron:

```
openstack network create test-vxlan-network
```

Verify that the network was created with the VXLAN type:

```
openstack network list --long
```

The output should indicate that the network is using VXLAN as the segmentation type.

In this recipe, we explored the different network types supported by Neutron, including flat networks, VLANs, VXLAN, and GRE. We assessed GitforGits' current network topology and determined that while VLAN is suitable for the present scale, transitioning to VXLAN would provide greater scalability and flexibility as the organization grows. We then reconfigured the network to use VXLAN, ensuring that GitforGits can take full advantage of Neutron's capabilities for secure and scalable network management.

Recipe 2: Configuring Neutron Plugins and

Agents

Introduction to Neutron Plugins and Agents

In Neutron, plugins and agents enables and manages network services. Plugins are responsible for managing the various networking features, such as L2 and L3 networking, security groups, and DHCP, while agents are responsible for implementing these services on the physical or virtual network infrastructure.

There are different types of plugins and agents in Neutron, each catering to specific network functions and backends. The most commonly used plugins include the Modular Layer 2 (ML2) plugin, which supports a variety of network types and mechanisms, and the L3 plugin, which manages routing between networks. Agents, on the other hand, are services that run on compute and network nodes to handle tasks such as configuring network interfaces, managing virtual switches, and implementing security rules.

For GitforGits, configuring the appropriate Neutron plugins and agents is essential for ensuring that the network functions required by the organization are properly supported and managed. In this recipe, we will configure the necessary Neutron plugins and agents to enable and manage the network features required for GitforGits' cloud environment.

A quick overview of Neutron Plugins and Agents:

Modular Layer 2 (ML2) Plugin

The ML2 plugin is the most commonly used Neutron plugin, supporting a variety of L2 network types, including VLAN, VXLAN, and GRE. It is highly modular, allowing different mechanisms to be plugged in, such as Open vSwitch (OVS) and LinuxBridge.

The ML2 plugin is suitable for environments that require flexibility in choosing different network technologies and mechanisms.

L3 Plugin

The L3 plugin is responsible for managing routing between different networks, enabling inter-network communication, and handling floating IPs for external access. It also manages distributed virtual routing (DVR) for high availability and scalability.

The L3 plugin is essential for environments that require routing capabilities, such as connecting private networks to external networks.

DHCP Agent

The DHCP agent manages DHCP services for tenant networks, providing IP address allocation to instances. It ensures that instances receive the correct IP addresses and network configurations when they are launched.

The DHCP agent is required in any environment where automatic IP address allocation is needed for instances.

Metadata Agent

The metadata agent serves instance metadata to instances, allowing them to retrieve configuration details such as SSH keys and user data. It works in conjunction with the DHCP agent and L3 agent to ensure that instances receive the necessary metadata.

The metadata agent is needed in environments where instances require access to metadata for initialization and configuration.

Open vSwitch (OVS) Agent

The OVS agent manages the configuration of virtual switches on compute and network nodes, handling tasks such as creating and managing VLANs and VXLAN tunnels.

The OVS agent is commonly used in environments that leverage Open vSwitch for network connectivity and isolation.

LinuxBridge Agent

The LinuxBridge agent manages network bridges on compute and network nodes using the LinuxBridge technology. It is an alternative to the OVS agent for environments that prefer LinuxBridge over Open vSwitch.

The LinuxBridge agent is suitable for simpler environments that do not require the advanced features of Open vSwitch.

Configuring Neutron Plugins and Agents

In this, we will configure the ML2 plugin with the OVS agent, along with the L3, DHCP, and metadata agents. This setup provides a robust and scalable network architecture that supports VLAN and VXLAN, with the necessary services for routing, IP address management, and instance metadata.

Configure the ML2 Plugin

Edit the ML2 configuration file (**/etc/neutron/plugins/ml2/ml2_conf.ini**) to enable the required mechanisms and network types:

```
sudo nano /etc/neutron/plugins/ml2/ml2_conf.ini
```

Update the configuration as follows:

```
[ml2]

type_drivers = vlan,vxlan
```

```
tenant_network_types = vxlan

mechanism_drivers = openvswitch


[ml2_type_vlan]

network_vlan_ranges = physnet1:100:200


[ml2_type_vxlan]

vni_ranges = 1000:5000


[ovs]

bridge_mappings = physnet1:br-ex
```

In the above script,

- **type_drivers**: Specifies the network types supported (VLAN and VXLAN).

- **tenant_network_types**: Defines the default network type for tenant networks (VXLAN).

- **mechanism_drivers**: Specifies the mechanism driver to be used (Open vSwitch).

- **network_vlan_ranges**: Defines the VLAN ID range for VLAN networks.

- **vni_ranges**: Defines the VXLAN Network Identifier (VNI) range for VXLAN networks.

- **bridge_mappings**: Maps the physical network interface to the Open vSwitch bridge.

Configure the OVS Agent

Configure the Open vSwitch (OVS) agent to manage the virtual switches on the compute and network nodes. Edit the OVS agent configuration file (**/etc/neutron/plugins/ml2/openvswitch_agent.ini**):

```
sudo nano /etc/neutron/plugins/ml2/openvswitch_agent.ini
```

Update the configuration as follows:

```
[ovs]

local_ip = <compute_node_ip>

tunnel_types = vxlan

bridge_mappings = physnet1:br-ex


[agent]

tunnel_types = vxlan
```

Configure the L3 Agent

The L3 agent is responsible for routing and managing external networks. Edit the L3 agent configuration file (**/etc/neutron/l3_agent.ini**):

```
sudo nano /etc/neutron/l3_agent.ini
```

Update the configuration as follows:

```
[DEFAULT]

interface_driver = openvswitch

external_network_bridge = br-ex
```

Here,

- **interface_driver**: Specifies the interface driver to be used (Open vSwitch).
- **external_network_bridge**: Specifies the bridge used for external networks.

Configure the DHCP Agent

The DHCP agent manages DHCP services for tenant networks. Edit the DHCP agent configuration file (**/etc/neutron/dhcp_agent.ini**):

```
sudo nano /etc/neutron/dhcp_agent.ini
```

Update the configuration as follows:

```
[DEFAULT]

interface_driver = openvswitch

dhcp_driver = neutron.agent.linux.dhcp.Dnsmasq
```

Configure the Metadata Agent

The metadata agent serves instance metadata to instances. Edit the metadata agent configuration file (**/etc/neutron/metadata_agent.ini**):

```
sudo nano /etc/neutron/metadata_agent.ini
```

Update the configuration as follows:

```
[DEFAULT]

nova_metadata_ip = <controller_ip>

metadata_proxy_shared_secret = <metadata_secret>
```

Replace **<controller_ip>** with the IP address of the controller node and **<metadata_secret>** with a secure shared secret for the metadata proxy.

Starting and Verifying Neutron Services

Start the Neutron Services

After configuring the plugins and agents, start the Neutron services on the controller and compute nodes:

```
sudo systemctl restart neutron-server
```

```
sudo systemctl restart neutron-openvswitch-agent

sudo systemctl restart neutron-l3-agent

sudo systemctl restart neutron-dhcp-agent

sudo systemctl restart neutron-metadata-agent
```

Verify the Configuration

Verify that the Neutron services are running correctly and that the network functions are operational:

```
openstack network agent list
```

This command should list all the Neutron agents (OVS, L3, DHCP, Metadata) with their statuses as "up." This confirms that the agents are properly configured and communicating with the Neutron server.

Test Network Functionality

Create a test network and subnet in Neutron to verify that the network is functioning as expected:

```
openstack network create test-network

openstack subnet create --network test-network --subnet-
range 10.0.0.0/24 test-subnet
```

Then, launch an instance and check that it receives an IP address from the DHCP agent and can access the metadata service.

In this recipe, we configured Neutron plugins and agents for GitforGits, ensuring that the cloud environment has the necessary networking capabilities to support its operations. This configuration enables robust network segmentation, routing, and IP address management, providing a scalable and flexible network architecture.

Recipe 3: Setting up Neutron L2 Networking (VLAN, VXLAN)

Previously, we introduced the concept of L2 networking and explored various network types supported by Neutron, including VLAN and VXLAN. We learned that L2 networking creates isolated segments within a cloud environment, allowing instances to communicate within the same network segment while maintaining isolation from other segments. VXLAN, in particular, was discussed as an advanced network type that extends the VLAN ID space by encapsulating L2 frames within UDP packets, enabling large-scale network segmentation.

Now, we will build on that foundation by diving into the practical setup of L2 networking with VLAN and VXLAN in the GitforGits environment. This recipe will guide you through the steps to create and manage these networks, ensuring proper connectivity and isolation for instances.

Setting up VLAN Networking

VLAN (Virtual LAN) is a network segmentation method that uses the IEEE 802.1Q standard to tag traffic on different virtual networks over a single physical network. VLANs provide secure isolation between different network segments while sharing the same physical infrastructure.

Create a VLAN Network

To create a VLAN network in Neutron, specify the VLAN ID and physical network. Ensure that the VLAN ID falls within the range configured in the ML2 plugin (**/etc/neutron/plugins/ml2/ml2_conf.ini**).

```
openstack network create --provider-network-type vlan --
provider-physical-network physnet1 --provider-segment 101
--share vlan-network-101
```

In the above script,

- **--provider-network-type vlan**: Specifies the network type as VLAN.

- **--provider-physical-network physnet1**: Indicates the physical network to which the VLAN is mapped.

- **--provider-segment 101**: Assigns VLAN ID 101 to the network.

- **--share**: Makes the network accessible to other projects (optional).

Create a Subnet for the VLAN Network

After creating the VLAN network, create a subnet to allocate IP addresses to instances on this network:

```
openstack subnet create --network vlan-network-101 --
subnet-range 192.168.101.0/24 vlan-subnet-101
```

Here,

- **--network vlan-network-101**: Associates the subnet with the VLAN network.

- **--subnet-range 192.168.101.0/24**: Specifies the IP address range for the subnet.

Launch an Instance on the VLAN Network

Launch an instance and associate it with the VLAN network to verify connectivity:

```
openstack server create --flavor m1.small --image
<image_id> --network vlan-network-101 --key-name mykey
vlan-instance-1
```

The instance should receive an IP address from the VLAN subnet and be isolated from other networks.

Verify VLAN Connectivity

SSH into the instance and test connectivity within the VLAN network:

```
ssh -i mykey.pem ubuntu@192.168.101.10
```

Verify that instances on the same VLAN network can communicate with each other but are isolated from other VLANs or networks.

Setting up VXLAN Networking

VXLAN (Virtual Extensible LAN) extends VLAN's functionality by encapsulating L2 frames within UDP packets, allowing for scalable network segmentation across different physical and virtual environments. VXLAN supports a much larger number of segments (up to 16 million), making it ideal for large-scale, multi-tenant environments.

Create a VXLAN Network

To create a VXLAN network, specify the VXLAN network type and a VNI (VXLAN Network Identifier). The VNI should fall within the range configured in the ML2 plugin

(**/etc/neutron/plugins/ml2/ml2_conf.ini**).

```
openstack network create --provider-network-type vxlan --
provider-segment 1001 --share vxlan-network-1001
```

Here,

- **--provider-network-type vxlan**: Specifies the network type as VXLAN.
- **--provider-segment 1001**: Assigns VNI 1001 to the network.
- **--share**: Makes the network accessible to other projects (optional).

Create a Subnet for the VXLAN Network

After creating the VXLAN network, create a subnet to allocate IP addresses to instances on this network:

```
openstack subnet create --network vxlan-network-1001 --
subnet-range 10.0.100.0/24 vxlan-subnet-1001
```

Launch an Instance on the VXLAN Network

Launch an instance and associate it with the VXLAN network to verify connectivity:

```
openstack server create --flavor m1.small --image
<image_id> --network vxlan-network-1001 --key-name mykey
vxlan-instance-1
```

The instance should receive an IP address from the VXLAN subnet.

Verify VXLAN Connectivity

SSH into the instance and test connectivity within the VXLAN network:

```
ssh -i mykey.pem ubuntu@10.0.100.10
```

Verify that instances on the same VXLAN network can communicate with each other across different physical hosts, thanks to VXLAN's encapsulation.

In this recipe, we built on our understanding of L2 networking and VXLAN by setting up and configuring both VLAN and VXLAN networks in the GitforGits environment.

Recipe 4: Implementing Neutron L3 Routing

Introduction to Neutron L3 Routing

In cloud environments, Layer 3 (L3) routing is essential for enabling communication between different networks. Neutron L3 routing facilitates the routing of traffic between subnets, networks, and external networks, allowing instances on different networks to communicate with each other and with external networks like the internet. This capability connects private networks to external resources, managing floating IPs, and providing internet access to instances.

In this recipe, we will explore how to implement Neutron L3 routing in the GitforGits environment. We will configure routers, connect internal networks, set up external networks, and assign floating IPs to instances. This will enable GitforGits to create a fully functional, routed network topology that supports both internal and external communication.

Before setting up L3 routing, we need to configure an external network in Neutron. The external network represents the network that provides connectivity to the outside world, such as the internet.

Create the External Network

To create an external network, use the following command:

```
openstack network create --external --provider-network-
type flat --provider-physical-network physnet1 external-
network
```

Here,

- **--external**: Marks the network as external.

- **--provider-network-type flat**: Specifies the network type as flat, which is typical for external networks.

- **--provider-physical-network physnet1**: Maps the network to the physical network interface.

Create a Subnet for the External Network

Next, create a subnet for the external network. This subnet should have a range of IP addresses that are routable and accessible from outside the cloud environment.

```
openstack subnet create --network external-network --
subnet-range 203.0.113.0/24 --allocation-pool
start=203.0.113.100,end=203.0.113.200 --gateway
203.0.113.1 --no-dhcp external-subnet
```

In the above code,

- **--subnet-range 203.0.113.0/24**: Specifies the IP address range for the external subnet.

- **--allocation-pool**: Defines the range of IP addresses available for floating IPs.

- **--gateway 203.0.113.1**: Sets the gateway IP address for the external subnet.

- **--no-dhcp**: Disables DHCP on the external network since external IPs are typically statically assigned.

Creating and Configuring Router

With the external network in place, the next step is to create a router in Neutron. The router will route traffic between internal networks and the external network, enabling communication between instances on different networks and providing external connectivity.

Create a Router

Create a new router using the following command:

```
openstack router create gitforgits-router
```

This command creates a router named **gitforgits-router**.

Set the External Gateway for the Router

Set the external network as the gateway for the router. This allows the router to route traffic from internal networks to the external network:

```
openstack router set gitforgits-router --external-gateway
external-network
```

This command configures the router to use the **external-network** as its gateway.

Connect Internal Networks to the Router

Connect the internal networks (e.g., VLAN or VXLAN networks) to the router. This allows instances on these networks to communicate with each other and access external networks through the router.

```
openstack router add subnet gitforgits-router vlan-
subnet-101

openstack router add subnet gitforgits-router vxlan-
subnet-1001
```

These commands connect the vlan-subnet-101 and vxlan-subnet-1001 to the gitforgits-router.

Assigning Floating IPs to Instances

Floating IPs allow instances on internal networks to be accessible from external networks. This is particularly useful for providing public access to web servers, SSH access to instances, and other use cases where external connectivity is required.

Allocate a Floating IP

Allocate a floating IP from the external network:

```
openstack floating ip create external-network
```

The command returns a floating IP address that you can associate with an instance.

Associate the Floating IP with an Instance

Associate the floating IP with an instance to make it accessible from the external network:

```
openstack server add floating ip vlan-instance-1
<floating_ip>
```

This command makes the **vlan-instance-1** instance accessible from the external network via the floating IP.

Verify External Connectivity

Test external connectivity by accessing the instance via the floating IP. You should be able to SSH into the instance or access services running on it:

```
ssh -i mykey.pem ubuntu@<floating_ip>
```

This confirms that the instance is successfully connected to the external network through the router.

Implementing Advanced L3 Features

Neutron's L3 agent also supports advanced features such as Distributed Virtual Routing (DVR) and High Availability (HA) routers, which can be implemented based on GitforGits' needs.

Enable DVR in the ML2 Configuration

Edit the ML2 configuration file (**/etc/neutron/plugins/ml2/ml2_conf.ini**) and enable DVR:

```
[ml2]

mechanism_drivers = openvswitch,l2population


[agent]

enable_distributed_routing = True

l3_ha = True
```

This configuration enables distributed routing and high availability for the L3 agent.

Enable DVR for the Router

To use DVR, you need to create a DVR-enabled router:

```
openstack router create --distributed gitforgits-dvr-router
```

This command creates a router with DVR enabled.

Configuring High Availability (HA) Routers

HA routers provide redundancy by deploying multiple instances of the router on different nodes. If the primary router fails, a backup router takes over, ensuring continuous network connectivity.

To use HA, create a router with high availability enabled:

```
openstack router create --ha gitforgits-ha-router
```

This command creates a high-availability router.

In this recipe, we implemented Neutron L3 routing to enable communication between internal networks and external networks in the GitforGits environment. By following these steps, you can ensure seamless and scalable network connectivity for your cloud infrastructure to have secure and efficient communication across all components of the environment.

Recipe 5: Configuring Neutron Security Groups and Firewall Rules

Security Groups and Firewall Rules

In modern cloud environments, security is a paramount concern, especially when it comes to protecting networked resources. Neutron security groups and firewall rules provide a robust mechanism for controlling traffic to and from instances, ensuring that only authorized connections are allowed. Security groups act as virtual firewalls that filter incoming and outgoing traffic at the instance level, while firewall rules provide additional layers of security at the network level.

The recent trends in cloud security have highlighted the increasing sophistication of network-based attacks, including distributed denial-of-service (DDoS) attacks, lateral movement within networks, and targeted exploits against cloud instances. To counter these threats, security groups and firewall rules must be meticulously configured to minimize attack surfaces while maintaining necessary connectivity. The security best practices now recommend adopting a "zero trust" model, where the default posture is to deny all traffic unless explicitly permitted. This approach reduces the likelihood of unauthorized access and limits the potential damage of compromised instances. Additionally, cloud environments are increasingly leveraging automated tools to manage and enforce security policies across dynamic and scalable infrastructures, ensuring consistent security posture even as the environment evolves.

In this recipe, we will explore how to configure Neutron security groups and firewall rules in the GitforGits environment. We will implement security best practices to protect instances and networks from unauthorized access while ensuring that necessary services remain accessible.

Understanding Neutron Security Groups

Security groups in Neutron are sets of IP filter rules that define the allowed inbound and outbound traffic for instances. Each instance can be associated with one or more security groups, and the rules within these groups determine what traffic is permitted to and from the instance.

By default, every OpenStack project has a security group named **default**. This group allows all outbound traffic but denies all inbound traffic unless explicitly permitted. It is a good practice to modify this group or create custom security groups tailored to specific applications and use cases. It is often useful to create custom security groups that are specific to the roles and functions of different instances. For example, a security group for web servers might allow HTTP and HTTPS traffic, while a security group for database servers might restrict access to only certain IP ranges.

Configuring Neutron Security Groups

- Create a Custom Security Group

To create a custom security group for the GitforGits environment, use the following command:

```
openstack security group create gitforgits-web-sg --
description "Security group for GitforGits web servers"
```

This command creates a security group named **gitforgits-web-sg** with a description indicating its purpose.

- Add Inbound Rules to the Security Group

Next, add rules to allow inbound traffic for HTTP (port 80) and HTTPS (port 443), which are commonly used for web servers:

```
openstack security group rule create --proto tcp --dst-
port 80 --ingress --description "Allow HTTP traffic"
gitforgits-web-sg

openstack security group rule create --proto tcp --dst-
port 443 --ingress --description "Allow HTTPS traffic"
gitforgits-web-sg
```

These commands add rules to the **gitforgits-web-sg** security group, permitting inbound HTTP and HTTPS traffic.

- Add Outbound Rules to the Security Group

By default, outbound traffic is usually allowed, but you can explicitly define outbound rules if needed. For example, to restrict outbound traffic to only allow DNS queries:

```
openstack security group rule create --proto udp --dst-
port 53 --egress --description "Allow DNS queries"
gitforgits-web-sg
```

This rule allows instances in the **gitforgits-web-sg** security group to perform DNS queries.

- Associate the Security Group with an Instance

Finally, associate the security group with an instance to apply the rules:

```
openstack server add security group <instance_name>
gitforgits-web-sg
```

This command applies the **gitforgits-web-sg** security group to the specified instance.

Configuring Firewall Rules

In addition to security groups, Neutron can be configured with firewall rules at the network level. These rules can be used to control traffic between networks or to implement more granular security policies that complement security groups.

- Enable and Configure the Neutron Firewall Service

If the firewall service (such as Firewall-as-a-Service, FWaaS) is not already enabled, you need to enable it in the Neutron configuration. Edit the Neutron configuration file (**/etc/neutron/neutron.conf**) and add the following:

```
[fwaas]

enabled = True

driver = iptables
```

Then, restart the Neutron service to apply the changes:

```
sudo systemctl restart neutron-server
```

- Create a Firewall Policy

A firewall policy is a collection of firewall rules that are applied to a network. First, create a firewall policy:

```
openstack firewall group policy create gitforgits-fw-
policy --description "Firewall policy for GitforGits"
```

This command creates a firewall policy named **gitforgits-fw-policy**.

- Add Rules to the Firewall Policy

Add rules to the firewall policy to control traffic between networks. For example, to allow SSH traffic from a specific IP range:

```
openstack firewall rule create --protocol tcp --
destination-port 22 --source-ip-address 192.168.1.0/24 --
action allow --name allow-ssh

openstack firewall group policy insert rule allow-ssh
gitforgits-fw-policy
```

This command creates a rule named **allow-ssh** that permits SSH traffic from the **192.168.1.0/24** network and adds it to the **gitforgits-fw-policy**.

- Apply the Firewall Policy to a Network

Finally, apply the firewall policy to a network by creating a firewall group and associating it with the policy:

```
openstack firewall group create --ingress-firewall-policy
gitforgits-fw-policy --name gitforgits-fw-group

openstack firewall group set --port <router_port_id>
gitforgits-fw-group
```

This command ensures that traffic passing through the router is filtered according to the firewall policy.

Best Practices for Security Groups and Firewall Rules

- Start with a default deny-all rule and explicitly allow only the traffic that is necessary. This minimizes the attack surface and reduces the risk of unauthorized access.

- Periodically review security groups and firewall rules to ensure they are still relevant and aligned with the organization's security policies. Remove or update rules that are no longer needed.

- Use clear and descriptive names and descriptions for security groups, firewall policies, and rules. This makes it easier to manage and audit the security configurations.

- Enable logging for security group and firewall rule actions, and monitor traffic patterns for signs of unauthorized access or potential security incidents.

In this recipe, we started by discussing recent insights into cloud security, emphasizing the need for a "zero trust" approach and the increasing use of automated tools to manage security. We then demonstrated how to configure security groups and firewall rules in the GitforGits environment, providing practical steps to create, manage, and apply these security measures effectively.

Recipe 6: Troubleshooting Neutron Networking Issues

In cloud environments managed by OpenStack, networking is one of the most critical and complex components. As we've learned through the previous recipes in this chapter, setting up and configuring Neutron for various networking tasks—such as L2 and L3 networking, security groups, and firewall rules—requires careful attention to detail. However, even with the best configurations, issues can arise that disrupt network connectivity or degrade performance. Troubleshooting these issues effectively provides a stable and secure cloud environment.

In this recipe, we will explore the most common networking issues that might arise while working through the previous recipes and provide practical, hands-on solutions. By understanding these troubleshooting techniques, GitforGits can ensure that its OpenStack environment remains reliable and responsive, even in the face of networking challenges.

Troubleshooting L2 Networking Issues (VLAN, VXLAN)

Instances on the Same VLAN/VXLAN Cannot Communicate

Instances on the same VLAN or VXLAN network are unable to ping each other or access shared services.

Possible Causes:

- Misconfiguration of the VLAN ID or VXLAN Network Identifier (VNI).

- Incorrect physical network mappings or bridge configurations.

- Open vSwitch (OVS) agent not running or misconfigured.

Solution:

- Verify VLAN/VXLAN Configuration

Check that the correct VLAN ID or VNI is configured in Neutron and on the physical switches or routers:

```
openstack network show <network_id>
```

Verify that the **provider:segmentation_id** matches the expected VLAN ID or VNI.

- Check Bridge Mappings

Ensure that the OVS bridge mappings are correctly configured on the compute and network nodes:

```
sudo ovs-vsctl show
```

Verify that the physical network interfaces are correctly mapped to the OVS bridges (e.g., **br-ex**).

- Restart the OVS Agent

If the OVS agent is not functioning correctly, restart it:

```
sudo systemctl restart neutron-openvswitch-agent
```

Check the OVS agent logs (**/var/log/neutron/openvswitch-agent.log**) for errors.

High Latency or Packet Loss in VXLAN Networks

Instances on VXLAN networks experience high latency or intermittent packet loss.

Possible Causes:

- CPU overhead due to VXLAN encapsulation.
- Network congestion or insufficient bandwidth.
- Incorrect MTU (Maximum Transmission Unit) settings.

Solution:

- Check MTU Settings

VXLAN encapsulation adds overhead to packets, which can cause issues if the MTU is not correctly set. Ensure that the MTU is configured correctly on the VXLAN networks:

```
openstack network show <vxlan_network_id>
```

Verify that the MTU is set to 1450 or lower to account for the VXLAN overhead.

- Monitor Network Traffic

Use tools like **iftop** or **vnstat** to monitor network traffic and identify potential bottlenecks or congestion on the physical network interfaces.

- Optimize VXLAN Performance

Consider enabling hardware offloading for VXLAN processing on network interfaces that support it, which can reduce CPU overhead and improve performance.

Troubleshooting L3 Routing Issues

Instances Cannot Reach External Networks

Instances on internal networks are unable to access external networks or the internet, even though a router is configured.

Possible Causes:

- Misconfiguration of the router's external gateway.
- Incorrect routing tables or missing default route.
- Floating IPs not associated or incorrectly configured.

Solution:

- Verify Router Configuration

Check that the router's external gateway is correctly set:

```
openstack router show <router_id>
```

Ensure that the **external_gateway_info** is set and points to the correct external network.

- Check Routing Tables

On the instance, check the routing table to ensure that there is a default route pointing to the Neutron router:

```
ip route
```

If the default route is missing, verify that the DHCP agent is correctly assigning routes.

- Test Floating IP Connectivity

If a floating IP is assigned, ensure it is correctly associated with the instance:

```
openstack floating ip list
```

Verify that the floating IP is associated with the correct instance and that security groups allow the necessary traffic.

Intermittent Connectivity Between Internal Networks

Instances on different internal networks intermittently lose connectivity, or there is a delay in establishing connections.

Possible Causes:

- Issues with the L3 agent or distributed routing (DVR) setup.

- Asymmetric routing due to misconfiguration of the external gateway.

- Network congestion or firewall rule conflicts.

Solution:

- Check L3 Agent Logs

Review the L3 agent logs for errors or issues related to routing:

```
tail -f /var/log/neutron/l3-agent.log
```

Look for any errors related to the router or network interfaces.

- Verify DVR Configuration

If using DVR, ensure that it is correctly configured on all relevant nodes. Check the OVS and L3 agent configurations to verify that distributed routing is properly set up.

- Monitor Network Traffic and Congestion

Use network monitoring tools to identify potential congestion or bottlenecks that could be affecting routing performance. Consider implementing Quality of Service (QoS) policies to prioritize critical traffic.

Troubleshooting Security Groups and Firewall Rules

Instances Not Accessible Despite Correct Security Group Rules

Instances are not accessible via SSH, HTTP, or other services, even though security group rules are correctly configured.

Possible Causes:

- Misconfigured firewall rules on the host or network nodes.
- Security group rules not applied due to Neutron agent issues.
- Conflicting rules between security groups and firewall policies.

Solution:

- Verify Security Group Rules

Double-check the security group rules to ensure they are correctly configured:

```
openstack security group show <security_group_id>
```

Ensure that the necessary inbound and outbound rules are present and correctly specified.

- Check Neutron Logs for Errors

Review the Neutron server and agent logs for any errors related to security group rule application:

```
tail -f /var/log/neutron/neutron-server.log

tail -f /var/log/neutron/iptables-firewall.log
```

Look for any errors that indicate issues with security group rule application.

- Test with a Different Security Group

As a troubleshooting step, create a new security group with minimal rules (e.g., allow all inbound traffic) and apply it to the instance to see if the issue persists. This can help determine if the issue is with the security group configuration or elsewhere.

Firewall Rules Blocking Legitimate Traffic

Certain legitimate traffic is being blocked by firewall rules, preventing instances from communicating as expected.

Possible Causes

- Overly restrictive firewall rules.
- Firewall policy conflicts or misconfigurations.
- Incorrect order of firewall rules leading to unintended blocking.

Solution:

- Review Firewall Policies and Rules:

Check the firewall policies and rules to ensure they are not overly restrictive or conflicting with each other:

```
openstack firewall group policy show <policy_id>
```

Review the order of the rules to ensure that allow rules are prioritized correctly.

- Log Dropped Packets

Enable logging for dropped packets to identify which rules are blocking legitimate traffic. Adjust the firewall rules accordingly to allow necessary traffic.

- Temporarily Disable Specific Rules

As a diagnostic step, disable specific firewall rules temporarily to see if the issue resolves. This can help pinpoint which rule is causing the issue:

```
openstack firewall rule delete <rule_id>
```

After identifying the problematic rule, adjust it to allow legitimate traffic while maintaining security.

In this recipe, we focused on troubleshooting the most common Neutron networking issues that might arise while performing the tasks covered in the previous recipes. We explored solutions for issues related to L2 and L3 networking, security groups, and firewall rules. These troubleshooting skills are essential for managing a reliable cloud infrastructure and quickly resolving any issues that may arise.

Recipe 7: Integrating Neutron with SDN Controllers

Integrating Neutron with an SDN controller can greatly enhance the networking capabilities of your cloud environment, providing advanced features such as automated network provisioning, real-time traffic management, and improved security through dynamic policy enforcement.

Here, we will assume the use of the OpenDaylight (ODL) SDN controller, a popular open-source platform that integrates well with OpenStack. In this recipe, we will demonstrate the steps to integrate Neutron with OpenDaylight, enabling advanced SDN features within the GitforGits environment.

Overview of OpenDaylight

OpenDaylight (ODL) is an open-source SDN controller platform that provides a flexible, modular framework for managing network devices and services. It offers a variety of networking protocols, including OpenFlow, NETCONF, and BGP, and is capable of controlling both physical and virtual network infrastructure. By integrating ODL with Neutron, you can leverage its centralized control and automation capabilities to manage complex network topologies, optimize traffic flows, and enforce security policies across the GitforGits cloud environment.

Preparing Integration

Before integrating Neutron with OpenDaylight, ensure that the following prerequisites are met:

- Install OpenDaylight

OpenDaylight should be installed and running on a dedicated server or virtual machine. You can download and install OpenDaylight from the official OpenDaylight website.

```
wget
https://nexus.opendaylight.org/content/repositories/opend
aylight-
release/org/opendaylight/integration/distribution-
karaf/0.8.4-Boron-SR4/distribution-karaf-0.8.4-Boron-
SR4.tar.gz

tar -xzf distribution-karaf-0.8.4-Boron-SR4.tar.gz

cd distribution-karaf-0.8.4-Boron-SR4

./bin/karaf
```

Once installed, start the OpenDaylight service and verify that it is running.

- Install Neutron ML2 Plugin for OpenDaylight

On the OpenStack controller node, install the Neutron ML2 plugin for OpenDaylight:

```
sudo apt-get install neutron-server neutron-plugin-ml2-
networking-odl
```

This plugin allows Neutron to communicate with the OpenDaylight controller.

Configuring Neutron to use OpenDaylight

Modify the Neutron ML2 Configuration

Edit the ML2 configuration file (**/etc/neutron/plugins/ml2/ml2_conf.ini**) to configure Neutron to use the OpenDaylight mechanism driver:

```
sudo nano /etc/neutron/plugins/ml2/ml2_conf.ini
```

Update the configuration as follows:

```
[ml2]

type_drivers = vlan,vxlan

tenant_network_types = vxlan

mechanism_drivers = opendaylight


[ml2_odl]

url =
http://<odl_controller_ip>:8080/controller/nb/v2/neutron

username = admin

password = admin
```

In the above script,

- **mechanism_drivers**: Set this to **opendaylight** to use the OpenDaylight mechanism driver.

- **url**: Specify the URL of the OpenDaylight controller's Neutron northbound API.

- **username** and **password**: Provide the OpenDaylight controller's admin credentials.

Modify the Neutron Server Configuration

Edit the Neutron server configuration file (**/etc/neutron/neutron.conf**) to integrate with OpenDaylight:

```
sudo nano /etc/neutron/neutron.conf
```

Update the configuration as follows:

```
[DEFAULT]

core_plugin = ml2

service_plugins = odl-router


[odl]

url =
http://<odl_controller_ip>:8080/controller/nb/v2/neutron

username = admin

password = admin
```

In this code,

- **core_plugin**: Set this to **ml2** to use the ML2 plugin with OpenDaylight.
- **service_plugins**: Include **odl-router** to use OpenDaylight for L3 routing.

After updating the configuration files, restart the Neutron services to apply the changes:

```
sudo systemctl restart neutron-server

sudo systemctl restart neutron-openvswitch-agent

sudo systemctl restart neutron-l3-agent
```

This ensures that Neutron is now integrated with OpenDaylight and ready to manage the network using the SDN controller.

Verifying Integration

- Check OpenDaylight Controller Dashboard

Access the OpenDaylight web-based dashboard by navigating to `http://<odl_controller_ip>:8181` in your web browser. Log in with the admin credentials.

Verify that the Neutron networks, subnets, and ports are visible in the OpenDaylight dashboard, indicating that Neutron is successfully communicating with the SDN controller.

- Create and Manage Networks via OpenDaylight

Create a new network and subnet in OpenStack and verify that it appears in OpenDaylight:

```
openstack network create odl-test-network

openstack subnet create --network odl-test-network --subnet-range 192.168.50.0/24 odl-test-subnet
```

Check the OpenDaylight dashboard to ensure that the network and subnet are listed.

- Test Instance Connectivity

Launch an instance on the newly created network and verify that it has network connectivity managed by OpenDaylight:

```
openstack server create --flavor m1.small --image <image_id> --network odl-test-network --key-name mykey odl-test-instance
```

Test the instance's connectivity to other instances or external networks to ensure that OpenDaylight is correctly managing the network flows.

In this recipe, we integrated Neutron with the OpenDaylight SDN controller to achieve greater flexibility, scalability, and control over the network infrastructure to better meet the demands of a dynamic cloud environment in future.

Summary

In a nutshell, the chapter started off with a review of various types of networks, such as virtual local area networks (VLANs) and virtual Xenon (VXLANs), including the configurations and use cases associated with each of these types of networks. The process of configuring L2 networking was detailed, allowing for the use of VLAN and VXLAN networks to enable network segmentation and isolation. L3 routing was then covered, including how to configure routers, connect internal networks, and enable external connectivity with floating IP addresses. This chapter focused heavily on security, providing a detailed explanation of how to configure Neutron security groups and firewall rules to protect instances and networks from unauthorized access and potential threats.

The chapter addressed common Neutron networking issues and provided practical solutions to problems that may arise during the implementation of L2 and L3 networking, security groups, and firewall configurations. Finally, the integration of Neutron with an SDN controller, namely OpenDaylight, was investigated. This included setting up Neutron to work with the SDN controller and utilizing advanced SDN features such as automated network provisioning, dynamic traffic management, and security policy enforcement. These lessons provided you with the knowledge and skills required to effectively manage and secure your cloud networking infrastructure.

CHAPTER 5: COMPUTE RESOURCES WITH NOVA

Introduction

In this chapter, we will look at the core of OpenStack compute resources by exploring the capabilities of Nova, the compute service that powers the creation and management of virtual machine instances. The goal of this chapter is to provide you the tools you need to manage and scale instances in your OpenStack environment, as well as deploy them. Each recipe in this chapter is designed to provide practical, hands-on experience with Nova, allowing you to confidently manage compute resources in a variety of scenarios.

Every OpenStack administrator needs to know how to use Nova to launch virtual machine instances, so that's where we start. Following that, we manage instance placement and affinity rules, which are critical for optimizing resource usage and ensuring that workloads are strategically placed based on your infrastructure's requirements. We'll also go over deploying instances with SSH key injection, which is an important aspect of securing access to your virtual machines. The next section tackles Nova hypervisors and how to use various hypervisors, such as KVM and QEMU, to control the execution and management of instances. And lastly, you'll also learn how to set up Nova for resource quotas and limits, ensuring that your cloud environment remains efficient and within operational parameters.

Recipe 1: Launching Virtual Machine Instances with Nova

Nova Overview

Nova is the core compute service in OpenStack, responsible for managing the lifecycle of virtual machine (VM) instances. It acts as the primary interface between the cloud's compute resources and the users who need to deploy and manage these VMs. For GitforGits, Nova offers essential features such as on-demand provisioning of instances, automated resource scheduling, and seamless integration with other OpenStack services like Neutron for networking and Cinder for storage. This makes Nova a needed component in ensuring that the compute infrastructure is scalable, flexible, and efficient.

In this recipe, we will focus on launching virtual machine instances using Nova within the GitforGits environment. We'll go through the practical steps required to deploy a VM instance, including selecting an appropriate flavor, configuring network connectivity, and ensuring secure access via SSH. These tasks are fundamental for managing compute resources and form the foundation for more advanced operations with Nova.

Selecting Flavor

A flavor in OpenStack defines the compute, memory, and storage capacity of a virtual machine instance. For GitforGits, selecting the right flavor matches the resource needs of different workloads.

- List Available Flavors

To see the flavors available in your OpenStack environment, run the following command:

```
openstack flavor list
```

Review the output to select a flavor that meets the needs of your workload. For example, **m1.small** might be a suitable flavor for a development server with minimal resource requirements.

- Create a Custom Flavor

If none of the existing flavors meet your requirements, you can create a custom flavor:

```
openstack flavor create --ram 4096 --vcpus 2 --disk 20
custom-flavor
```

This command creates a flavor with 4 GB of RAM, 2 VCPUs, and 20 GB of disk space, named **custom-flavor**.

Launching VM Instance

With the flavor selected, you can now launch a VM instance using Nova.

- Launch an Instance

Use the following command to create a new VM instance:

```
openstack server create --flavor m1.small --image
<image_id> --network <network_id> --key-name mykey --
security-group <security_group_name> gitforgits-instance1
```

This command instructs Nova to create a new virtual machine instance using the specified flavor, image, and network.

- Monitor the Instance Launch

After issuing the command, monitor the status of the instance to ensure it launches successfully:

```
openstack server list
```

The status should change from **BUILD** to **ACTIVE**, indicating that the instance has been successfully launched.

Accessing the Instance

Once the instance is active, you can access it via SSH using the key pair specified during the instance creation.

- Retrieve the Instance's IP Address

Use the **openstack server list** command to retrieve the IP address assigned to the instance:

```
openstack server list
```

Note the IP address associated with the instance under the **Networks** column.

- SSH into the Instance

Access the instance using SSH:

```
ssh -i mykey.pem ubuntu@<instance_ip>
```

If the image uses a different default user (e.g., **centos** for CentOS images), adjust the SSH command accordingly.

Verifying Instance Functionality

- Check Instance Resources

Once logged in, verify that the instance has been allocated the correct resources (CPU, RAM, disk) based on the selected flavor:

```
free -m

df -h

lscpu
```

These commands provide details about the memory, disk space, and CPU configuration of the instance.

- Test Network Connectivity

Verify that the instance can reach other instances and external networks (if configured). Test this by pinging an external IP or another instance within the same network:

```
ping <another_instance_ip>
```

```
ping 8.8.8.8
```

Successful pings confirm that the instance's networking is properly configured.

In this recipe, we walked through the process of launching a virtual machine instance, including selecting a flavor, configuring networking, and securing access with SSH key injection. By following these steps, you've successfully deployed a virtual machine instance in the GitforGits environment, thereby setting the stage for more advanced Nova functionalities that we'll cover in the upcoming recipes.

Recipe 2: Managing Instance Placement and Affinity Rules

In the previous recipe, we focused on launching VM instances using Nova within the GitforGits environment. We covered the steps necessary to choose the right flavor, configure networking, and secure access to the instances. Now that you have successfully launched a VM instance, it's time to explore how you can control the placement of these instances on the available compute nodes in your OpenStack cloud. This is where instance placement strategies and affinity rules come into play.

Affinity and Anti-Affinity Rules

Affinity and anti-affinity rules are policies that guide how instances are placed on physical hosts within your OpenStack environment. These rules are essential for optimizing resource utilization, improving performance, and ensuring fault tolerance.

- **Affinity Rules**: Affinity rules ensure that certain instances are placed on the same host. This is useful in scenarios where instances need to be close to each other to reduce latency, share resources, or communicate more efficiently.

- **Anti-Affinity Rules**: Anti-affinity rules, on the other hand, ensure that certain instances are placed on different hosts. This is necessary for high availability and fault tolerance, as it prevents a single point of failure. For example, if two instances are critical to an application, placing them on different hosts ensures that if one host fails, the other instance remains unaffected.

These rules allow GitforGits to manage its infrastructure more effectively, whether it's by ensuring that critical services are distributed across multiple hosts or by placing related services together to minimize network latency.

Defining Instance Placement Strategies

Before diving into the practical implementation, it's important to understand how instance placement strategies can be defined in OpenStack. Placement strategies are dictated by scheduler hints, which are key-value pairs that influence where an instance will be placed. These hints can be used to enforce both affinity and anti-affinity rules.

- **Scheduler Hints**: Scheduler hints are additional metadata that can be passed during the instance creation process. These hints inform the Nova scheduler about specific placement preferences.

- **Aggregate Metadata**: Placement decisions can also be influenced by setting metadata on host aggregates (groups of compute nodes) to ensure that instances are placed on nodes that meet certain criteria, such as having specific hardware characteristics or being located in a particular data center.

Implementing Affinity Rules

Let's assume that GitforGits wants to ensure that a set of instances that work closely together (e.g., a web server and its corresponding application server) are placed on the same compute node to reduce latency.

Creating an Affinity Group

Nova supports the concept of server groups, which are used to apply affinity or anti-affinity policies. To create an affinity group, use the following command:

```
openstack server group create --policy affinity
gitforgits-affinity-group
```

This command creates a server group named **gitforgits-affinity-group** with an affinity policy, meaning that all instances added to this group will be placed on the same compute node.

Launching Instances with Affinity

When launching instances that should adhere to this affinity policy, you need to specify the server group using the **--hint** option:

```
openstack server create --flavor m1.small --image
<image_id> --network <network_id> --key-name mykey --
security-group <security_group_name> --hint
group=<server_group_id> gitforgits-web-instance1
```

Replace **<server_group_id>** with the ID of the **gitforgits-affinity-group**
created in the previous step. Launch another instance in the same group to see them placed on
the same host:

```
openstack server create --flavor m1.small --image
<image_id> --network <network_id> --key-name mykey --
security-group <security_group_name> --hint
group=<server_group_id> gitforgits-app-instance1
```

Both instances will be scheduled to the same host, adhering to the affinity policy.

Verifying Affinity Placement

To verify that the instances have been placed on the same compute node, you can use the
openstack server show command to check the **OS-EXT-SRV-ATTR:host** attribute
for both instances:

```
openstack server show gitforgits-web-instance1
```

```
openstack server show gitforgits-app-instance1
```

Both instances should show the same host under the **OS-EXT-SRV-ATTR:host** attribute,
confirming that they were placed together.

Implementing Anti-Affinity Rules

Now, consider a scenario where GitforGits needs to deploy instances that provide redundancy
for critical services, such as two database instances. To ensure high availability, these instances
should be placed on different compute nodes.

Creating an Anti-Affinity Group

Similar to affinity, you can create a server group with an anti-affinity policy:

```
openstack server group create --policy anti-affinity
gitforgits-anti-affinity-group
```

This command creates a server group named **gitforgits-anti-affinity-group** with an anti-affinity policy, ensuring that instances in this group are placed on different compute nodes.

Launching Instances with Anti-Affinity

When launching instances that should adhere to this anti-affinity policy, specify the server group in the **--hint** option:

```
openstack server create --flavor m1.small --image
<image_id> --network <network_id> --key-name mykey --
security-group <security_group_name> --hint
group=<server_group_id> gitforgits-db-instance1
```

Launch another instance in the same group to ensure they are placed on different hosts:

```
openstack server create --flavor m1.small --image
<image_id> --network <network_id> --key-name mykey --
security-group <security_group_name> --hint
group=<server_group_id> gitforgits-db-instance2
```

These instances will be placed on different hosts, adhering to the anti-affinity policy.

Verifying Anti-Affinity Placement

Similar to the affinity policy, you can verify that the instances are placed on different hosts by checking the **OS-EXT-SRV-ATTR:host** attribute:

```
openstack server show gitforgits-db-instance1
```

```
openstack server show gitforgits-db-instance2
```

The **OS-EXT-SRV-ATTR:host** attribute should show different hosts for each instance, confirming that the anti-affinity policy is in effect.

Managing and Modifying Affinity Rules

Once affinity or anti-affinity rules are set, there might be a need to modify or delete these rules as the infrastructure evolves. GitforGits might require changing the server group policies or moving instances to different server groups based on changing workload requirements.

Revising Server Group Policies

If you need to change the policy of an existing server group (e.g., from affinity to anti-affinity), you will need to create a new server group with the desired policy, as policies cannot be changed once set.

```
openstack server group create --policy anti-affinity
gitforgits-revised-group
```

Then, migrate the instances from the old group to the new group by re-launching them under the new group.

If you need to add or remove instances from a server group, this can be done by launching new instances with the desired group or deleting instances that should no longer adhere to the group's policy.

Adding an Instance

Launch a new instance with the desired server group:

```
openstack server create --flavor m1.small --image
<image_id> --network <network_id> --key-name mykey --
security-group <security_group_name> --hint
group=<server_group_id> gitforgits-new-instance
```

Removing an Instance

To remove an instance from a server group, you will need to delete it and re-launch it without the **--hint** option or with a different group.

Deleting a Server Group

If a server group is no longer needed, you can delete it:

```
openstack server group delete <server_group_id>
```

This will remove the server group, but note that it does not automatically affect the placement of instances that were created under this group.

Advanced Placement Strategies

In addition to affinity and anti-affinity rules, Nova allows for more granular control over instance placement through the use of host aggregates and availability zones.

- **Host Aggregates**: Host aggregates allow you to group compute nodes with similar characteristics (e.g., SSD storage, high memory) and apply metadata to these groups. You can then use this metadata to influence where instances are placed based on their resource needs.

- **Availability Zones**: Availability zones are logical groupings of hosts that provide an additional layer of fault tolerance. Instances can be placed in different availability zones to ensure they are isolated from failures in other zones.

Creating a Host Aggregate

Create a host aggregate and assign metadata to it:

```
openstack aggregate create gitforgits-ssd-aggregate

openstack aggregate set --property ssd=true gitforgits-
ssd-aggregate
```

Add hosts to this aggregate:

```
openstack aggregate add host gitforgits-ssd-aggregate
<host_name>
```

Instances with specific requirements can now be scheduled to this aggregate by specifying the appropriate metadata in the scheduler hints.

Using Availability Zones

Create an availability zone and place instances accordingly:

```
openstack availability zone list
```

Launch instances in a specific availability zone by specifying the zone:

```
openstack server create --flavor m1.small --image
<image_id> --availability-zone <zone_name> --network
<network_id> --key-name mykey --security-group
<security_group_name> gitforgits-zone-instance
```

This ensures that the instance is placed within the desired availability zone, providing additional isolation from failures in other zones.

In this recipe, we extended the knowledge gained from launching VM instances, and introduced the concept of server groups, demonstrated how to implement these rules to optimize performance and ensure high availability, and discussed how to modify or delete these rules as your infrastructure needs evolve. Additionally, we touched on advanced placement strategies using host aggregates and availability zones to further refine control over instance placement.

Recipe 3: Deploying Instances with SSH Key Injection

SSH Keys for Deploying Instances

SSH (Secure Shell) key injection is a fundamental security practice when deploying VM instances in cloud environments. The use of SSH keys rather than passwords for instance access is highly recommended due to the enhanced security and convenience it offers. An SSH key pair consists of a public key and a private key. The public key is injected into the instance at the time of creation, while the private key remains with the user. This setup eliminates the need for password authentication, making it much harder for attackers to gain unauthorized access.

The main advantages of using SSH keys for deploying instances include:

- **Enhanced Security**: Unlike passwords, which can be guessed or brute-forced, SSH keys provide a much stronger form of authentication. The private key is never exposed to the network, and since it is typically stored securely on the user's machine, the risk of compromise is significantly reduced.

- **Convenience and Automation**: Once SSH key pairs are set up, users can access their instances without needing to enter a password. This is particularly useful in environments where multiple instances need to be accessed or managed frequently. Additionally, SSH keys facilitate automation, allowing scripts and tools to interact with instances securely and without manual intervention.

- **Centralized Key Management**: In cloud environments, managing SSH keys centrally through services like OpenStack makes it easier to enforce security policies and manage access control. Administrators can quickly revoke or update keys across multiple instances, reducing the risk of unauthorized access.

Given these benefits, SSH key injection is a critical part of deploying instances securely in the GitforGits environment. In this recipe, we will demonstrate how to deploy instances with SSH key injection using Nova, ensuring that all instances are accessible securely and efficiently.

Creating an SSH Key Pair

Before deploying an instance with SSH key injection, you need to generate an SSH key pair. If you already have an SSH key pair, you can skip this step.

Generate a New SSH Key Pair

On your local machine, you can generate a new SSH key pair using the following command:

```
ssh-keygen -t rsa -b 4096 -C "gitforgits-key"
```

This command generates a 4096-bit RSA key pair. During the process, you will be prompted to specify a file name and location to save the key. The default location is **~/.ssh/id_rsa**. You can name the key **gitforgits-key** or any other name you prefer.

After the key pair is generated, you will have two files:

- **~/.ssh/gitforgits-key**: The private key, which should be kept secure and never shared.
- **~/.ssh/gitforgits-key.pub**: The public key, which can be distributed and injected into instances.

Upload the Public Key to OpenStack

The next step is to upload the public key to OpenStack, so it can be used during instance deployment:

```
openstack keypair create --public-key ~/.ssh/gitforgits-key.pub gitforgits-key
```

This command uploads the public key to OpenStack under the name **gitforgits-key**. This key will now be available for use when launching instances.

Launching an Instance with SSH Key Injection

With the SSH key pair ready and uploaded to OpenStack, you can now launch an instance with SSH key injection.

165

Launch the Instance

Use the following command to create a new VM instance with the SSH key injected:

```
openstack server create --flavor m1.small --image
<image_id> --network <network_id> --key-name gitforgits-
key --security-group <security_group_name> gitforgits-
ssh-instance
```

This command tells Nova to launch the instance with the **gitforgits-key** injected, allowing you to access the instance securely via SSH.

Monitor the Instance Launch

After issuing the command, monitor the status of the instance to ensure it launches successfully:

```
openstack server list
```

The status should change from **BUILD** to **ACTIVE**, indicating that the instance has been successfully launched.

Accessing the Instance via SSH

Once the instance is active, you can access it using the SSH key pair you configured.

Retrieve the Instance's IP Address

Use the **openstack server list** command to retrieve the IP address assigned to the instance:

```
openstack server list
```

Note the IP address associated with the instance under the **Networks** column.

SSH into the Instance

Access the instance using the following SSH command:

```
ssh -i ~/.ssh/gitforgits-key ubuntu@<instance_ip>
```

If the connection is successful, you will have secure shell access to your instance, ready for further configuration and management.

Managing SSH Keys

As your infrastructure grows, you may need to manage multiple SSH keys, update keys, or revoke access for certain users. OpenStack provides straightforward commands for these tasks.

Listing SSH Keys

To list all SSH keys associated with your OpenStack account, use the following command:

```
openstack keypair list
```

This will display all the key pairs you have uploaded to OpenStack, along with their names and associated fingerprints.

Deleting an SSH Key

If an SSH key is no longer needed or if you want to revoke access, you can delete it from OpenStack:

```
openstack keypair delete gitforgits-key
```

This command removes the **gitforgits-key** from OpenStack. Any instances that were launched with this key will no longer have access via SSH unless another key is added or the instance is recreated.

Updating an SSH Key

If you need to update an SSH key (for example, if the private key has been compromised), you should first delete the old key and then upload a new one following the steps outlined earlier. After uploading the new key, you will need to update your instances with the new key by launching them again with the updated key name.

SSH Key Management Best Practices

To ensure security and efficient management of SSH keys within the GitforGits environment, consider the following best practices:

Always use strong key pairs, such as 4096-bit RSA keys or Ed25519 keys, to ensure robust encryption. Avoid using shorter keys or older algorithms like DSA, which are considered less secure.

Ensure that private keys are stored securely on your local machine. Use file permissions to restrict access, and consider using hardware security modules (HSMs) or other secure storage mechanisms for additional protection.

Periodically rotate SSH keys to minimize the risk of compromise. Regular rotation ensures that even if a key is compromised, its exposure is limited.

Assign SSH keys to specific users or instances based on their roles and responsibilities. Avoid using a single key pair across all instances, as this increases the risk if the key is compromised.

Regularly audit SSH key usage in your OpenStack environment. Keep track of which keys are in use, who has access to which instances, and ensure that old or unused keys are removed promptly.

In this recipe, we explored generating an SSH key pair and uploading it to OpenStack, followed by a step-by-step demonstration of how to launch an instance with the SSH key injected. We also covered how to access the instance securely via SSH and manage SSH keys within OpenStack, including best practices for key management.

Recipe 4: Using Nova Hypervisors (KVM, QEMU)

Nova Hypervisors: KVM and QEMU

The hypervisor is the core component that allows the creation and management of virtual machines (VMs). Nova interfaces with various hypervisors to deploy and manage these VMs. Two of the most widely used hypervisors in OpenStack environments are KVM (Kernel-based Virtual Machine) and QEMU (Quick Emulator).

- **KVM (Kernel-based Virtual Machine)**: KVM is a full virtualization solution for Linux on x86 hardware containing virtualization extensions (Intel VT or AMD-V). KVM converts the Linux kernel into a hypervisor, allowing it to run multiple isolated virtual environments called guests or VMs. KVM is integrated directly into the Linux kernel, making it a popular choice for OpenStack deployments due to its performance, stability, and strong security features. KVM requires hardware support for virtualization, which is available in most modern CPUs.

- **QEMU (Quick Emulator)**: QEMU is a generic and open-source machine emulator and virtualizer. When used in conjunction with KVM, QEMU provides the emulation of hardware devices and enables the execution of guest code at near-native speed. QEMU can operate in two modes: as a full emulator (where it simulates a full system) or as a hypervisor (when paired with KVM). QEMU's versatility makes it a valuable tool in scenarios where full hardware emulation is necessary, although it is typically slower when running in pure emulation mode compared to KVM.

In this recipe, we will explore how to utilize KVM and QEMU within the GitforGits OpenStack environment, ensuring that our cloud infrastructure is optimized for performance, scalability, and flexibility.

Verifying Hypervisor Support

Before using KVM or QEMU, it's important to verify that your environment supports these hypervisors and that the necessary components are installed.

- Check for Hardware Virtualization Support

To check if your system supports hardware virtualization, run the following command:

```
egrep -c '(vmx|svm)' /proc/cpuinfo
```

If the output is greater than 0, your CPU supports hardware virtualization, which is required for KVM.

- Verify KVM Modules

Check if the KVM modules are loaded in the kernel:

```
lsmod | grep kvm
```

You should see **kvm** and **kvm_intel** (or **kvm_amd** for AMD processors) listed. If not, you may need to load the modules manually:

```
sudo modprobe kvm

sudo modprobe kvm_intel  # or kvm_amd for AMD processors
```

- Ensure QEMU is Installed

Verify that QEMU is installed on your compute nodes:

```
qemu-system-x86_64 --version
```

If QEMU is not installed, you can install it using your package manager:

```
sudo apt-get install qemu-kvm libvirt-bin bridge-utils
virt-manager
```

This installs QEMU along with KVM and other necessary tools.

Configuring Nova to Use KVM and QEMU

Nova needs to be configured to use KVM or QEMU as the hypervisor for launching instances. This configuration is done on the compute nodes.

- Edit the Nova Configuration File

Open the Nova configuration file (**/etc/nova/nova.conf**) on the compute node and ensure the following settings are applied:

```
sudo nano /etc/nova/nova.conf
```

In the **[libvirt]** section, configure the hypervisor type:

```
[libvirt]

virt_type = kvm  # Use 'qemu' if KVM is not supported or required

cpu_mode = host-passthrough
```

Here,

1. **virt_type**: Set this to **kvm** to use KVM. If your hardware does not support KVM, you can set this to **qemu** for full emulation.
2. **cpu_mode**: **host-passthrough** is recommended for performance, as it allows the guest to use the host's CPU features directly.

After making changes to the Nova configuration, restart the Nova compute service to apply the changes:

```
sudo systemctl restart nova-compute
```

This ensures that the changes take effect and Nova is now using the configured hypervisor.

Launching Instances with KVM or QEMU

With the hypervisor configured, you can now launch instances using Nova. By default, Nova will use the hypervisor configured on the compute node.

Launch an Instance

Use the following command to launch a new instance:

```
openstack server create --flavor m1.small --image
<image_id> --network <network_id> --key-name gitforgits-
key --security-group <security_group_name> gitforgits-
kvm-instance
```

This command launches an instance using the KVM or QEMU hypervisor, depending on your configuration.

Verify Hypervisor in Use

After the instance is launched, you can verify that it is running on the correct hypervisor by checking the instance's details:

```
openstack server show gitforgits-kvm-instance
```

Look for the **OS-EXT-SRV-ATTR:hypervisor_hostname** attribute, which should match the name of the compute node using the configured hypervisor.

Access the Instance

Once the instance is active, access it via SSH to ensure that it is functioning correctly:

```
ssh -i ~/.ssh/gitforgits-key ubuntu@<instance_ip>
```

Monitoring and Managing Hypervisors

Managing hypervisors in a production environment involves monitoring their performance, ensuring they are correctly configured, and maintaining their stability.

Monitor Hypervisor Performance

Use the following command to get an overview of the hypervisor's performance:

```
openstack hypervisor stats show
```

This command displays statistics such as the number of running VMs, CPU usage, memory usage, and disk usage.

List Hypervisors

To list all hypervisors available in your OpenStack environment, use:

```
openstack hypervisor list
```

This command provides details on all hypervisors, including their status and availability.

Migrate Instances

If necessary, you can migrate instances between hypervisors to balance the load or perform maintenance:

```
openstack server migrate <server_id>
```

This command initiates a live migration, moving the instance to another available hypervisor without downtime.

In this recipe, we explored the roles of KVM and QEMU as hypervisors in the Nova environment, understanding their strengths and use cases. We walked through the process of verifying hypervisor support, configuring Nova to use KVM or QEMU, and launching instances with these hypervisors. We also discussed performance considerations, monitoring hypervisor performance, and troubleshooting common issues.

Recipe 5: Configuring Nova for Resource Quotas and Limits

Resource Quotas and Limits in Nova

Resource quotas and limits are required for managing and controlling the allocation of compute resources across different projects. Quotas ensure that no single project or user can consume all available resources, thereby maintaining a balanced and fair usage of the cloud infrastructure. By configuring quotas, administrators can define the maximum number of instances, vCPUs, RAM, floating IPs, and other resources that can be allocated to a project. This is particularly important in multi-tenant environments where multiple teams or departments might share the same OpenStack environment.

In this recipe, we will explore how to configure and manage resource quotas and limits in Nova. We will also demonstrate how to allocate these resources project-wise, ensuring that each project within GitforGits has access to the necessary resources without exceeding the overall capacity of the cloud.

Understanding Default Quotas

OpenStack comes with a set of default quotas that apply to all projects unless overridden. These quotas include limits on the number of instances, vCPUs, RAM, floating IPs, and other resources.

To view the default quotas in Nova, use the following command:

```
openstack quota show --default
```

This command will display the default quotas for various resources such as instances, cores (vCPUs), RAM, and more. For example:

```
+------------------------------+-------+
| Field                        | Value |
+------------------------------+-------+
| cores                        | 20    |
| instances                    | 10    |
| ram                          | 51200 |
| floating_ips                 | 10    |
| security_groups              | 10    |
| security_group_rules         | 100   |
+------------------------------+-------+
```

These values represent the maximum resources that any single project can consume by default.

Configuring Custom Quotas

To tailor resource allocation according to the needs of specific projects within GitforGits, you can modify the default quotas on a per-project basis.

First, identify the project for which you want to set custom quotas. You can list all projects using:

```
openstack project list
```

This command will display a list of projects along with their IDs, which you will need for the next steps.

- Set Custom Quotas

To set custom quotas for a specific project, use the following command:

```
openstack quota set --cores 50 --instances 25 --ram
102400 --floating-ips 20 --security-groups 20
<project_id>
```

This above command sets custom quotas for the specified project. These quotas override the default values for this particular project.

- Verify the Quotas

After setting the custom quotas, verify them using:

```
openstack quota show <project_id>
```

This command displays the current quotas for the specified project, confirming that the custom quotas have been applied.

Managing Quota Allocations Across Multiple Projects

In a multi-tenant environment, it's demanding to manage quota allocations across multiple projects to ensure fair resource distribution and avoid overallocation.

- List Quotas for All Projects

To get an overview of quota allocations across all projects, you can use the following script or loop in your OpenStack environment:

```
for project in $(openstack project list -f value -c ID);
do
    echo "Quotas for project $project:"
    openstack quota show $project
    echo "---------------------------"
done
```

This loop iterates through all projects and displays their quotas, helping you assess the resource distribution.

- Adjust Quotas Based on Usage

If certain projects are consistently underutilizing or overutilizing their quotas, you may need to adjust their allocations. You can use the **openstack quota set** command to increase or decrease quotas based on actual usage patterns.

For example, to reduce the RAM quota for a project that is underutilizing its allocated memory:

```
openstack quota set --ram 51200 <project_id>
```

This command reduces the RAM quota to 50 GB for the specified project.

- Enforcing Hard Limits

In some cases, you may want to enforce hard limits on resource usage to prevent projects from requesting additional resources. OpenStack does this automatically based on the quotas you set. If a project tries to exceed its allocated resources, Nova will deny the request, ensuring that no project can consume more than its fair share of resources.

Monitoring and Managing Quota Usage

To effectively manage resources, it's important to monitor quota usage regularly. This allows you to anticipate when a project might need additional resources or when limits should be tightened.

Use the following command to monitor quota usage for a specific project:

```
openstack usage show <project_id>
```

This command provides detailed information about the project's resource usage, including the number of instances, vCPUs, RAM, and more.

For a more detailed view over a specific time period, you can use:

```
openstack usage list --project <project_id> --start
<start_date> --end <end_date>
```

Here, replace **<start_date>** and **<end_date>** with the desired time range in **YYYY-MM-DD** format. This helps in tracking resource consumption trends over time.

Setting Global Quotas

In some cases, you may want to set or adjust global quotas that apply to all projects unless overridden. This is useful for establishing baseline resource allocation across the environment.

You can use the following command to set global quotas:

```
openstack quota set --cores 1000 --instances 500 --ram
204800 --floating-ips 50 --security-groups 50 --default
```

This above command sets new global default quotas for all projects:

- **--cores 1000**: Limits total vCPUs across all projects.

- **--instances 500**: Limits the total number of instances across all projects.

- **--ram 204800**: Limits total RAM across all projects to 200 GB.

- **--floating-ips 50**: Limits the number of floating IPs across all projects.

Recipe 6: Automating Instance Deployments

Instance Deployment Automation

Manually deploying instances, as we've done in previous recipes, provides a deep understanding of the process and control over individual configurations. However, in a production environment where scalability and efficiency are key, automation becomes essential. Automating instance deployments not only saves time but also ensures consistency, reduces errors, and allows for rapid scaling of resources.

The Nova CLI offers powerful tools for automating these deployments and with the help of scripting commands and using Nova's batch capabilities, you can streamline the process of launching instances, managing configurations, and scaling resources. In this recipe, we'll explore how to automate the deployment of instances that were previously deployed manually. We'll also cover how to automate the deployment of multiple instances simultaneously, which is particularly useful for environments requiring quick scaling or load balancing.

Scripting a Single Instance Deployment

To begin with, we'll automate the deployment of a single instance using the Nova CLI. This script will replicate the manual steps we performed earlier, but in an automated and repeatable manner.

Begin by creating a shell script that automates the deployment of an instance. You can use any text editor to create this script. For example:

```
nano deploy_instance.sh
```

In the script, include the following commands:

```bash
#!/bin/bash


# Variables

IMAGE_ID="<image_id>"

FLAVOR="m1.small"

NETWORK_ID="<network_id>"

KEY_NAME="gitforgits-key"

SECURITY_GROUP="default"

INSTANCE_NAME="gitforgits-automated-instance"


# Create the instance

openstack server create --flavor $FLAVOR --image
$IMAGE_ID --network $NETWORK_ID --key-name $KEY_NAME --
security-group $SECURITY_GROUP $INSTANCE_NAME


# Check the instance status

openstack server list | grep $INSTANCE_NAME
```

After creating the script, make it executable:

```bash
chmod +x deploy_instance.sh
```

Execute the script to deploy the instance:

```
./deploy_instance.sh
```

The script will automatically create a new instance with the specified parameters, similar to how you manually deployed instances in previous recipes. The instance name will be **gitforgits-automated-instance**, and the script will output the instance's status once it is created.

Automating the Deployment of Multiple Instances

In many scenarios, you may need to deploy multiple instances simultaneously. Automating this process can be done by extending the script to loop through the deployment process for several instances.

Here, you modify the existing script to deploy multiple instances. For example:

```bash
#!/bin/bash


# Variables
IMAGE_ID="<image_id>"

FLAVOR="m1.small"

NETWORK_ID="<network_id>"

KEY_NAME="gitforgits-key"

SECURITY_GROUP="default"

INSTANCE_COUNT=5  # Number of instances to deploy

BASE_INSTANCE_NAME="gitforgits-automated-instance"


# Loop to create multiple instances
for i in $(seq 1 $INSTANCE_COUNT); do

    INSTANCE_NAME="${BASE_INSTANCE_NAME}-${i}"
```

```
    openstack server create --flavor $FLAVOR --image
$IMAGE_ID --network $NETWORK_ID --key-name $KEY_NAME --
security-group $SECURITY_GROUP $INSTANCE_NAME

done


# Check the status of all instances

openstack server list | grep $BASE_INSTANCE_NAME
```

In this script, **INSTANCE_COUNT** is the number of instances you want to deploy. The script loops through the deployment process, creating instances named **gitforgits-automated-instance-1**, **gitforgits-automated-instance-2**, and so on.

Then, execute the script to deploy multiple instances:

```
./deploy_instance.sh
```

This will create the specified number of instances, each with its unique name. The script will then list all the deployed instances to verify their status.

Automating Post-Deployment Tasks

Automating the deployment process can also include post-deployment tasks such as associating floating IPs, configuring security groups, and injecting metadata or configuration scripts.

- Adding Floating IP Assignment

You can modify the script to automatically assign floating IPs to the instances:

```
# Assign a floating IP to each instance

for i in $(seq 1 $INSTANCE_COUNT); do

    INSTANCE_NAME="${BASE_INSTANCE_NAME}-${i}"

    FLOATING_IP=$(openstack floating ip create public -f
value -c floating_ip_address)
```

```
    openstack server add floating ip $INSTANCE_NAME
$FLOATING_IP

    echo "Assigned Floating IP $FLOATING_IP to
$INSTANCE_NAME"

done
```

This section of the script creates a new floating IP from the public network and associates it with each instance.

- Automating Security Group Rules

If specific security group rules are required for these instances, they can be added automatically as part of the deployment script:

```
# Add custom security group rules

openstack security group rule create --protocol tcp --
dst-port 22 --ingress --description "Allow SSH"
$SECURITY_GROUP

openstack security group rule create --protocol tcp --
dst-port 80 --ingress --description "Allow HTTP"
$SECURITY_GROUP
```

This ensures that each instance is correctly configured with the necessary security rules upon deployment.

- Injecting Metadata or Cloud-Init Scripts

If you need to run specific configuration tasks on each instance after it launches, you can use Cloud-Init to inject scripts or metadata:

```
USER_DATA_FILE="user_data.sh"  # Path to your Cloud-Init
script
```

```
openstack server create --flavor $FLAVOR --image
$IMAGE_ID --network $NETWORK_ID --key-name $KEY_NAME --
security-group $SECURITY_GROUP --user-data
$USER_DATA_FILE $INSTANCE_NAME
```

This example shows how to pass a Cloud-Init script during instance creation, automating configuration tasks such as software installation, updates, or custom setups.

Scaling Deployment with Nova CLI

For larger environments or specific use cases, GitforGits may need to deploy dozens or even hundreds of instances. The Nova CLI allows you to efficiently scale deployments, either by adjusting the script or using batch processing.

For very large deployments, consider breaking the deployment into batches to avoid overloading the compute resources:

```
BATCH_SIZE=10   # Number of instances per batch


for batch in $(seq 1 $((INSTANCE_COUNT / BATCH_SIZE)));
do

    for i in $(seq 1 $BATCH_SIZE); do

        INSTANCE_NAME="${BASE_INSTANCE_NAME}-
batch${batch}-instance${i}"

        openstack server create --flavor $FLAVOR --image
$IMAGE_ID --network $NETWORK_ID --key-name $KEY_NAME --
security-group $SECURITY_GROUP $INSTANCE_NAME &

    done

    wait  # Wait for the batch to complete before
starting the next

done
```

This script deploys instances in batches, with each batch launching simultaneously. The **wait** command ensures that each batch completes before starting the next, preventing resource contention.

If you need to scale instances dynamically based on demand, you can integrate your deployment scripts with OpenStack's autoscaling features (like Heat or external orchestration tools). For example, you could set up an autoscaling group that triggers instance deployments based on CPU load or network traffic.

Monitoring and Managing Automated Deployments

Once your automation scripts are in place, it's important to monitor the deployments and manage instances effectively.

- Monitoring Instance Status

After the deployment, monitor the status of the instances using:

```
openstack server list | grep $BASE_INSTANCE_NAME
```

This command checks the status of all instances deployed by the script, allowing you to verify that they are running as expected.

- Handling Failures

If an instance fails to deploy, the script can be modified to handle such cases, such as retrying the deployment or logging the failure:

```
if [ $? -ne 0 ]; then

    echo "Failed to deploy $INSTANCE_NAME. Retrying..."

    # Retry logic here

fi
```

This ensures that the deployment process is robust and can recover from errors.

- Automating Cleanup

If instances are no longer needed, you can automate their cleanup with a simple script:

```
for i in $(seq 1 $INSTANCE_COUNT); do
```

```
    INSTANCE_NAME="${BASE_INSTANCE_NAME}-${i}"

    openstack server delete $INSTANCE_NAME

    echo "Deleted $INSTANCE_NAME"
done
```

This script automates the deletion of all instances created by the previous script, ensuring that resources are freed up when no longer needed.

In this recipe, we created scripts to automate single and multiple instance deployments, incorporating post-deployment tasks such as floating IP assignment, security group configuration, and Cloud-Init script injection. Additionally, we explored batch processing for large-scale deployments and integrated automation with monitoring and error handling.

Summary

Finally, we mastered the art of optimizing and managing compute resources in Nova. The chapter began with Nova launching virtual machine instances, after which we looked at the process of manually deploying instances and the advantages of using SSH key injection to ensure secure access. We then learned how to manage instance placement and affinity rules, which allow us to control where instances are deployed in the cloud. This included setting up affinity and anti-affinity rules to improve performance and ensure high availability.

The chapter goes deeper into Nova hypervisors, particularly KVM and QEMU for operating virtual machines in OpenStack. We learned how to set up these hypervisors in the Nova environment for maximum efficiency and performance. Furthermore, we looked into configuring resource quotas and limits in Nova, which is critical for managing resource allocation across multiple projects in GitforGits. Custom quotas were established to ensure fair resource utilization and prevent overallocation. Automation was another key focus, and we learned how to use the Nova CLI to automate instance deployment. This included scripting single and multiple instance deployments, as well as implementing post-deployment tasks such as assigning floating IP addresses and configuring security groups.

CHAPTER 6: BLOCK STORAGE WITH CINDER

Introduction

The purpose of this chapter is to get you skilled with Cinder, OpenStack's block storage service, and how to manage it. This chapter will provide you with the practical skills needed to effectively manage and secure storage resources in an OpenStack environment. The upcoming recipes will teach you how to create and attach volumes to instances, allowing for persistent storage that remains intact even when instances are stopped or deleted.

We'll look at managing volume snapshots, which are an important feature for data protection and recovery. If something were to go wrong with your data, you could quickly restore it from a snapshot because they record the volume's condition at a specific moment in time. The chapter also discusses using Cinder for backup and restore operations, which ensures that your critical data can be securely stored and retrieved as needed.

As we progress, you'll learn how to configure Cinder to use various storage backends, such as LVM and Ceph, to optimize your storage infrastructure's performance, scalability, and redundancy. Another critical aspect we'll cover is automation, with a focus on using the Cinder CLI to automate volume management, streamline repetitive tasks, and increase efficiency. Finally, the chapter covers advanced topics such as creating bootable volumes for persistent instances and using volume encryption to protect sensitive data.

Recipe 1: Creating and Attaching Volumes to Instances

Overview

Block storage provides persistent storage that can be attached to instances, enabling them to store data beyond their lifecycle. Cinder is the service responsible for managing block storage. By creating and attaching volumes, you can ensure that your instances have the necessary storage for applications, databases, and other critical data. This recipe will guide you through the process of creating and attaching volumes to the instances used by GitforGits, focusing on handling complex storage needs, such as multiple volumes or large capacity volumes.

Creating a Volume in Cinder

- Determine the Storage Requirements

Before creating a volume, it's important to understand the storage requirements of your application. This includes the size of the volume, the type of storage backend (e.g., SSD, HDD), and any performance considerations. For this example, let's create a 100 GB volume for a database application that requires high performance.

- Create the Volume

Use the following command to create a volume in Cinder:

```
openstack volume create --size 100 --description
"Database Volume for GitforGits" gitforgits-db-volume
```

This command creates a 100 GB volume named **gitforgits-db-volume**. You can verify the creation of the volume by listing all volumes:

```
openstack volume list
```

The output should show the newly created volume with its status as **available**.

If your instance requires multiple volumes, you can repeat the process to create additional volumes. For example, create a 50 GB volume for log storage:

```
openstack volume create --size 50 --description "Log
Volume for GitforGits" gitforgits-log-volume
```

Attaching Volumes to an Instance

Once the volumes are created, the next step is to attach them to an instance. For this example, let's attach the **gitforgits-db-volume** and **gitforgits-log-volume** to an instance that we previously deployed.

- Identify the Instance

List the instances to identify the one you want to attach the volumes to:

```
openstack server list
```

Note the **ID** or **Name** of the instance to which the volumes will be attached.

- Attach the Database Volume

Use the following command to attach the **gitforgits-db-volume** to the instance:

```
openstack server add volume <instance_id_or_name>
gitforgits-db-volume
```

This command attaches the **gitforgits-db-volume** to the specified instance. You can verify the attachment by checking the instance details:

```
openstack server show <instance_id_or_name>
```

Look for the **os-extended-volumes:volumes_attached** attribute to confirm that the volume is attached.

- Attach the Log Volume

Similarly, attach the **gitforgits-log-volume** to the instance:

```
openstack server add volume <instance_id_or_name>
gitforgits-log-volume
```

This command attaches the **gitforgits-log-volume** to the same instance. Again, verify the attachment by reviewing the instance details.

Verifying Attached Volumes

After attaching the volumes, you should verify that they are recognized by the instance and are ready for use.

- Access the Instance

SSH into the instance to which the volumes were attached:

```
ssh -i ~/.ssh/gitforgits-key ubuntu@<instance_ip>
```

- List Attached Disks

On the instance, list the attached disks to verify that the volumes are present:

```
lsblk
```

The output should display the newly attached volumes as block devices, such as **/dev/vdb** and **/dev/vdc**. These devices correspond to the **gitforgits-db-volume** and **gitforgits-log-volume**.

- Format the Volumes

Before using the volumes, they need to be formatted and mounted:

```
sudo mkfs.ext4 /dev/vdb

sudo mkfs.ext4 /dev/vdc

sudo mkdir /mnt/dbdata

sudo mkdir /mnt/logdata
```

This command formats the volumes with the ext4 filesystem and also creates directories where the volumes will be mounted.

- Mount the Volumes

```
sudo mount /dev/vdb /mnt/dbdata

sudo mount /dev/vdc /mnt/logdata
```

This command mounts the gitforgits-db-volume to /mnt/dbdata and the gitforgits-log-volume to /mnt/logdata.

Then, check the mounted filesystems to confirm:

```
df -h
```

The output should show the volumes mounted at **/mnt/dbdata** and **/mnt/logdata**, with their respective capacities.

Automating Volume Management

To automate the attachment and management of volumes in future deployments, consider using Cloud-Init scripts in which create a Cloud-Init script to automate the process of attaching and configuring volumes during instance boot:

```
#!/bin/bash

mkfs.ext4 /dev/vdb

mkfs.ext4 /dev/vdc

mkdir /mnt/dbdata
```

```
mkdir /mnt/logdata

mount /dev/vdb /mnt/dbdata

mount /dev/vdc /mnt/logdata
```

Pass this script to the instance during creation using the **--user-data** option:

```
openstack server create --flavor m1.small --image
<image_id> --network <network_id> --key-name gitforgits-
key --security-group default --user-data myscript.sh
gitforgits-automated-instance
```

This automates the volume management process, ensuring that the volumes are ready for use as soon as the instance is up. This recipe or the process provides persistent storage to your instances, allowing them to handle data-intensive tasks and applications effectively.

Recipe 2: Managing Volume Snapshots for Data Protection

Volume Snapshots Overview

Volume snapshots are a powerful feature in Cinder that allows you to capture the state of a volume at a specific point in time, which is of prime importance for data protection, enabling you to quickly recover from accidental deletions, data corruption, or other unforeseen issues. Snapshots provide a way to back up your data without taking the volume offline. In this recipe, we will explore how to create, manage, and use snapshots for the volumes we've created and attached to instances so far.

Creating a Volume Snapshot

Identify Volume for Snapshot

Before creating a snapshot, identify the volume you wish to snapshot. For example, let's create a snapshot of the **gitforgits-db-volume** we created in the previous recipe.

List the available volumes to confirm the volume name or ID:

```
openstack volume list
```

This command lists all the volumes, allowing you to identify the correct one for snapshotting.

Create the Snapshot

To create a snapshot of the volume, use the following command:

```
openstack volume snapshot create --volume gitforgits-db-
volume --name gitforgits-db-snapshot --description
"Snapshot of GitforGits DB Volume"
```

Here,

- **--volume gitforgits-db-volume**: Specifies the volume for which the snapshot will be created.

- **--name gitforgits-db-snapshot**: Provides a name for the snapshot.

- **--description**: Adds a description for the snapshot.

This command then creates a snapshot named **gitforgits-db-snapshot** of the **gitforgits-db-volume**. You can monitor the creation process by listing the snapshots:

```
openstack volume snapshot list
```

The status should initially show as **creating** and change to **available** once the snapshot is completed.

Managing Volume Snapshots

Once you've created a snapshot, managing it becomes a need for maintaining an organized and efficient storage environment. This involves viewing, deleting, and restoring from snapshots as needed.

- Viewing Snapshot Details

To view detailed information about a specific snapshot, use:

```
openstack volume snapshot show gitforgits-db-snapshot
```

This command displays detailed information about the snapshot, including its size, creation date, and status. It helps you verify that the snapshot was created correctly and is ready for use.

- Deleting a Snapshot

If a snapshot is no longer needed, you can delete it to free up storage space:

```
openstack volume snapshot delete gitforgits-db-snapshot
```

This command deletes the **gitforgits-db-snapshot**, permanently removing the snapshot from the storage system. It's important to ensure that the snapshot is no longer needed before deletion, as this process cannot be undone.

- Restoring a Volume from a Snapshot

One of the primary uses of snapshots is to restore a volume to a previous state. To restore a volume from a snapshot, you can either create a new volume from the snapshot or replace the existing volume with the snapshot data.

- Creating a New Volume from a Snapshot

To create a new volume from the snapshot:

```
openstack volume create --snapshot gitforgits-db-snapshot
--size 100 --description "Restored DB Volume" gitforgits-
db-restored-volume
```

This above command then creates a new volume named **gitforgits-db-restored-volume**, identical to the original volume at the time of the snapshot.

- Replacing an Existing Volume with a Snapshot

If you need to revert the original volume to the snapshot state, you'll need to delete the original volume and recreate it from the snapshot:

```
openstack volume delete gitforgits-db-volume
```

Then, create a new volume from the snapshot using the same name:

```
openstack volume create --snapshot gitforgits-db-snapshot
--size 100 --description "Restored DB Volume" gitforgits-
db-volume
```

This process restores the volume to its state at the time of the snapshot, effectively reverting any changes made since the snapshot was taken.

Automating Snapshot Management

In environments where volumes are frequently updated or critical data is involved, automating snapshot management can ensure regular backups without manual intervention. You can schedule regular snapshot creation using cron jobs or other automation tools. Here's an example of a simple cron job that creates a snapshot of the **gitforgits-db-volume** every day at midnight:

First, open the crontab for editing:

```
crontab -e
```

Add the following line to schedule the snapshot creation:

```
0 0 * * * openstack volume snapshot create --volume
gitforgits-db-volume --name gitforgits-db-snapshot-$(date
+\%Y\%m\%d) --description "Daily Snapshot of GitforGits
DB Volume"
```

This cron job will create a snapshot with a timestamp in its name, making it easy to identify the date of each snapshot.

Now, to prevent the accumulation of too many snapshots, which can consume significant storage space, you can automate the deletion of older snapshots. For example, to delete snapshots older than 7 days, you can add another cron job:

```
0 1 * * * openstack volume snapshot list --format value -
-column ID --column Created_at | awk -v d=$(date -d "7
days ago" +\%Y-\%m-\%d) '$2 < d {print $1}' | xargs -I {}
openstack volume snapshot delete {}
```

This job runs daily at 1 AM and deletes snapshots older than 7 days, ensuring that your storage usage remains under control.

Recipe 3: Cinder for Backup and Restore Operations

In addition to snapshots, Cinder provides robust backup and restore functionality for protecting data against failures, corruption, or accidental deletions. Unlike snapshots, which are typically stored locally and capture the state of a volume at a specific point in time, backups are usually stored externally, offering an extra layer of protection. In this recipe, we'll demonstrate how to perform backup and restore operations on the volumes we previously created for GitforGits.

Creating Volume Backup

Before creating a backup, identify the volume you wish to back up. For example, let's create a backup of the **gitforgits-db-volume** that we worked with earlier.

List the available volumes to confirm the volume name or ID:

```
openstack volume list
```

This command lists all the volumes, allowing you to identify the correct one for backup. Now, to create a backup of the volume, use the following command:

```
openstack volume backup create --name gitforgits-db-
backup --description "Backup of GitforGits DB Volume"
gitforgits-db-volume
```

This command creates a backup named **gitforgits-db-backup** for the **gitforgits-db-volume**.

You can then monitor the backup creation process by listing the backups:

```
openstack volume backup list
```

The status should initially show as **creating** and change to **available** once the backup is completed.

Managing Volume Backups

Once the backup is created, you can manage it, including viewing details, deleting, or restoring from the backup.

- Viewing Backup Details

To view detailed information about a specific backup, use:

```
openstack volume backup show gitforgits-db-backup
```

This command displays detailed information about the backup, including its size, creation date, and status. It helps you verify that the backup was created correctly and is ready for use.

- Deleting a Backup

If a backup is no longer needed, you can delete it to free up storage space:

```
openstack volume backup delete gitforgits-db-backup
```

This command deletes the **gitforgits-db-backup**, permanently removing the backup from the storage system. Be sure that the backup is no longer needed before deletion, as this process cannot be undone.

Restoring a Volume from a Backup

The primary purpose of creating backups is to restore data when needed. Cinder makes it easy to restore a volume from a backup, either by creating a new volume from the backup or by overwriting an existing volume.

To restore a volume from a backup and create a new volume:

```
openstack volume create --backup gitforgits-db-backup --
size 100 --description "Restored DB Volume from Backup"
gitforgits-db-restored-from-backup
```

If you need to restore the original volume from the backup, you will first need to delete the existing volume and then restore it from the backup.

```
openstack volume delete gitforgits-db-volume
```

Then, create a new volume from the backup using the same name:

```
openstack volume create --backup gitforgits-db-backup --
size 100 --description "Restored DB Volume from Backup"
gitforgits-db-volume
```

This effectively restores the **gitforgits-db-volume** to its state at the time of the backup, allowing you to recover the data if the original volume was corrupted or lost.

Automating Backup Management

Similar to snapshots, you can schedule regular backups using cron jobs or other automation tools. Here's an example cron job that creates a backup of the **gitforgits-db-volume** every week:

Open the crontab for editing:

```
crontab -e
```

Add the following line to schedule the weekly backup:

```
0 2 * * 0 openstack volume backup create --name
gitforgits-db-backup-$(date +\%Y\%m\%d) --description
"Weekly Backup of GitforGits DB Volume" gitforgits-db-
volume
```

This cron job creates a new backup every Sunday at 2 AM, naming each backup with the date it was created. To prevent backups from consuming excessive storage, automate the deletion of older backups:

```
0 3 * * 0 openstack volume backup list --format value --
column ID --column Created_at | awk -v d=$(date -d "4
weeks ago" +\%Y-\%m-\%d) '$2 < d {print $1}' | xargs -I
{} openstack volume backup delete {}
```

This job runs every Sunday at 3 AM and deletes backups older than 4 weeks, ensuring that only recent backups are retained.

In this recipe, we covered creating backups, managing them, and restoring volumes from these backups, providing a robust method for protecting critical data in the GitforGits environment.

Recipe 4: Configuring Cinder to use Storage Backend

Cinder, the block storage service in OpenStack, is designed to work with a variety of storage backends, allowing administrators to optimize storage resources based on performance, scalability, and cost requirements. In the context of GitforGits, selecting and configuring the right storage backend ensures that the cloud environment meets the needs of its applications and users.

For GitforGits, we have previously chosen Ceph to be the preferred storage backend due to its scalability and reliability. We'll demonstrate how to configure Cinder to use Ceph as the storage backend.

Preparing Ceph Cluster

Before configuring Cinder, ensure that the Ceph cluster is properly set up and operational. This includes having the Ceph monitor nodes, OSDs (Object Storage Daemons), and the Ceph client installed on the Cinder node.

First, make sure that the Ceph cluster is healthy and operational:

```
ceph status
```

The output should indicate a healthy cluster with all OSDs up and running.

Then, on the Cinder node, install the Ceph client packages:

```
sudo apt-get install ceph ceph-common
```

This ensures that the Cinder node can communicate with the Ceph cluster.

Configuring Cinder to use Ceph

Now that the Ceph cluster is ready, we can configure Cinder to use it as the storage backend. For this, open the Cinder configuration file (**/etc/cinder/cinder.conf**) on the Cinder node:

```
sudo nano /etc/cinder/cinder.conf
```

Then, add or update the following sections to configure Ceph as the storage backend:

```
[DEFAULT]

enabled_backends = ceph



[ceph]
```

```
volume_driver = cinder.volume.drivers.rbd.RBDDriver

rbd_pool = volumes

rbd_ceph_conf = /etc/ceph/ceph.conf

rbd_user = cinder

rbd_secret_uuid = <uuid_of_the_ceph_secret>

volume_backend_name = ceph
```

Here,

- **enabled_backends = ceph**: Specifies that Ceph is the enabled backend.
- **volume_driver**: Sets the driver to **RBDDriver** for Ceph's RADOS Block Device (RBD).
- **rbd_pool = volumes**: Specifies the Ceph pool used for Cinder volumes.
- **rbd_ceph_conf = /etc/ceph/ceph.conf**: Points to the Ceph configuration file.
- **rbd_user = cinder**: Specifies the Ceph user for Cinder.
- **rbd_secret_uuid = <uuid_of_the_ceph_secret>**: References the secret UUID for authentication (more on this below).
- **volume_backend_name = ceph**: Names the backend, used when configuring multiple backends.

Later, on the Ceph monitor node, create a Ceph user for Cinder:

```
ceph auth get-or-create client.cinder mon 'allow r' osd
'allow class-read object_prefix rbd_children, allow rwx
pool=volumes'
```

This command creates a user **client.cinder** with permissions to read and write to the **volumes** pool.

Following this, generate a UUID for the secret key:

```
uuidgen
```

Note the UUID, as it will be used in the Cinder configuration. On the Ceph monitor node, generate the key for the **cinder** user:

```
ceph auth get-key client.cinder | sudo tee
/etc/ceph/client.cinder.keyring
```

Create a secret in OpenStack to store the key:

```
sudo virsh secret-define --file
/etc/ceph/client.cinder.keyring

sudo virsh secret-set-value --secret
<uuid_of_the_ceph_secret> --base64 $(ceph auth get-key
client.cinder)
```

Replace **<uuid_of_the_ceph_secret>** with the UUID generated earlier. After updating the configuration, restart the Cinder services to apply the changes:

```
sudo systemctl restart cinder-volume

sudo systemctl restart cinder-scheduler
```

This ensures that Cinder is now using Ceph as its storage backend.

Verifying the Configuration

To ensure that the configuration is correct and Cinder is using the Ceph backend, perform the following checks:

- Create a Test Volume

Create a test volume to verify that Cinder is using the Ceph backend:

```
openstack volume create --size 10 test-volume
```

This command creates a 10 GB volume named **test-volume**. If the configuration is correct, the volume will be created in the Ceph cluster.

- Check the Ceph Cluster for the Volume

On the Ceph monitor node, check that the volume has been created in the Ceph pool:

```
rados -p volumes ls | grep volume
```

You should see an entry corresponding to the **test-volume**, indicating that the volume was successfully created in the Ceph backend.

- Attach the Volume to an Instance

As a final test, attach the volume to an instance:

```
openstack server add volume <instance_name_or_id> test-volume
```

Verify that the volume is attached and accessible from within the instance. With this, we demonstrated how to configure Cinder to use a specific storage backend, focusing on setting up Ceph for the GitforGits environment. We covered the necessary steps to integrate Cinder with Ceph, from configuring the Cinder service to creating and verifying volumes in the Ceph cluster.

Recipe 5: Automating Volume Management with Cinder CLI

While manual management of volumes is feasible in smaller setups, automation becomes essential as the environment grows. The Cinder CLI offers powerful commands that allow administrators to automate various volume management tasks, such as creating, attaching, detaching, and deleting volumes. In this recipe, we'll explore how to use the Cinder CLI to automate these tasks, improving efficiency and reducing the potential for human error.

Automate Volume Creation

Automating volume creation can save time, especially when provisioning multiple volumes for different instances or projects. To begin with. start by creating a simple shell script to automate the creation of multiple volumes.

```
nano create_volumes.sh
```

Add the following content to the script:

```bash
#!/bin/bash

# Variables

VOLUME_SIZE=50  # Size of each volume in GB

VOLUME_COUNT=5  # Number of volumes to create

BASE_VOLUME_NAME="gitforgits-volume"


# Loop to create multiple volumes

for i in $(seq 1 $VOLUME_COUNT); do

    VOLUME_NAME="${BASE_VOLUME_NAME}-${i}"

    openstack volume create --size $VOLUME_SIZE --
description "Automated Volume $i for GitforGits"
$VOLUME_NAME

    echo "Created volume $VOLUME_NAME"

done
```

This script creates five volumes, each 50 GB in size, with names like **gitforgits-volume-1**, **gitforgits-volume-2**, and so on. After saving the script, make it executable:

```
chmod +x create_volumes.sh
```

Execute the script to create the volumes:

```
./create_volumes.sh
```

The script will automatically create the specified number of volumes and display their creation status.

Automating Volume Attachment

Automating the attachment of volumes to instances can be useful when deploying multiple instances that each require their own storage. First, create a shell script to automate the attachment of the volumes created in the previous step to specific instances:

```
nano attach_volumes.sh
```

Add the following content to the script:

```bash
#!/bin/bash


# Variables

INSTANCE_ID="<instance_id>"  # Replace with the actual
instance ID

BASE_VOLUME_NAME="gitforgits-volume"

VOLUME_COUNT=5  # Number of volumes to attach


# Loop to attach each volume to the instance

for i in $(seq 1 $VOLUME_COUNT); do

    VOLUME_NAME="${BASE_VOLUME_NAME}-${i}"

    openstack server add volume $INSTANCE_ID $VOLUME_NAME

    echo "Attached $VOLUME_NAME to instance $INSTANCE_ID"
done
```

Replace **<instance_id>** with the actual ID of the instance you want to attach the volumes to.

```
chmod +x attach_volumes.sh
```

Execute the script to attach the volumes to the specified instance:

```
./attach_volumes.sh
```

The script will attach each volume to the instance, displaying the status of each operation.

Automating Volume Detachment and Deletion

Volume detachment and deletion are equally important tasks that can also be automated to ensure that unused resources are freed up promptly. Here, to automate the detachment of volumes from an instance, create the following script:

```
nano detach_volumes.sh
```

Add the following content:

```bash
#!/bin/bash


# Variables

INSTANCE_ID="<instance_id>"  # Replace with the actual
instance ID

BASE_VOLUME_NAME="gitforgits-volume"

VOLUME_COUNT=5  # Number of volumes to detach


# Loop to detach each volume from the instance

for i in $(seq 1 $VOLUME_COUNT); do

    VOLUME_NAME="${BASE_VOLUME_NAME}-${i}"
```

```
    openstack server remove volume $INSTANCE_ID
$VOLUME_NAME

    echo "Detached $VOLUME_NAME from instance
$INSTANCE_ID"

done
```

Execute the script to detach the volumes:

```
./detach_volumes.sh
```

The script will detach each volume from the instance. After detaching volumes, you can automate their deletion with another script:

```
nano delete_volumes.sh
```

Add the following content:

```
#!/bin/bash


# Variables

BASE_VOLUME_NAME="gitforgits-volume"

VOLUME_COUNT=5  # Number of volumes to delete


# Loop to delete each volume

for i in $(seq 1 $VOLUME_COUNT); do

    VOLUME_NAME="${BASE_VOLUME_NAME}-${i}"

    openstack volume delete $VOLUME_NAME
```

```
        echo "Deleted volume $VOLUME_NAME"

done
```

This script will delete each of the specified volumes.

Scheduling Automated Tasks

To fully automate volume management tasks, consider scheduling these scripts to run at specific intervals using cron jobs. Here, to schedule the creation of volumes every Monday at midnight, add the following to your crontab:

```
crontab -e
```

Add:

```
0 0 * * 1 /path/to/create_volumes.sh
```

This ensures that the script runs automatically at the specified time. Also, to delete volumes automatically every Sunday at midnight:

```
0 0 * * 0 /path/to/delete_volumes.sh
```

This keeps your storage usage optimized by regularly removing unneeded volumes.

In this recipe, we demonstrated how to automate various volume management tasks using the Cinder CLI. We covered the automation of volume creation, attachment, detachment, and deletion, providing practical examples that can be adapted to the needs of GitforGits. Additionally, we explored how to schedule these tasks using cron jobs, ensuring that your storage environment is efficiently managed with minimal manual intervention.

Recipe 6: Implementing Volume Encryption for Data Security

Setting up Encryption Key Manager

Before you can implement volume encryption in Cinder, you need to have an encryption key manager configured. OpenStack typically uses Barbican to handle encryption keys.

- Install Barbican

If Barbican is not already installed, you can install it using the following commands:

```
sudo apt-get update

sudo apt-get install barbican-api barbican-keystone-
listener barbican-worker barbican-common
```

- Configure Barbican

After installation, configure Barbican by editing the **/etc/barbican/barbican.conf** file:

```
sudo nano /etc/barbican/barbican.conf
```

Ensure that the key manager section is configured correctly:

```
[keystone_authtoken]

auth_uri = http://<keystone-host>:5000

auth_url = http://<keystone-host>:35357

memcached_servers = <keystone-host>:11211

auth_type = password

project_domain_name = Default

user_domain_name = Default

project_name = service

username = barbican

password = <barbican-password>
```

Replace **<keystone-host>** with your Keystone host and **<barbican-password>** with the password for the Barbican user.

- Restart Barbican Services

Restart the Barbican services to apply the changes:

```
sudo systemctl restart barbican-api barbican-worker
barbican-keystone-listener
```

Creating an Encryption Type for Volumes

Now that Barbican is set up, you can create an encryption type that will be applied to the volumes in your GitforGits environment.

- Create an Encryption Type

Create an encryption type for the volume type you're using. First, list the existing volume types to choose the appropriate one:

```
openstack volume type list
```

Next, create an encryption type for the desired volume type. For example:

```
openstack volume type create --encryption-provider luks -
-name gitforgits-encrypted-volumes
```

This command creates a new volume type called **gitforgits-encrypted-volumes** with LUKS (Linux Unified Key Setup) as the encryption provider.

- Set Encryption Specifications

You can specify additional encryption details, such as cipher and key size, when creating the encryption type:

```
openstack volume type encryption set --provider luks --
cipher aes-xts-plain64 --key-size 256 --control-location
front-end gitforgits-encrypted-volumes
```

This command configures the encryption to use the AES cipher with a 256-bit key.

Creating and Attaching Encrypted Volumes

With the encryption type configured, you can now create and attach encrypted volumes to your instances.

- Create an Encrypted Volume

Use the following command to create a new encrypted volume:

```
openstack volume create --type gitforgits-encrypted-
volumes --size 100 --description "Encrypted Database
Volume" gitforgits-encrypted-db-volume
```

This command creates a 100 GB encrypted volume named **gitforgits-encrypted-db-volume**.

- Attach the Encrypted Volume to an Instance

Attach the newly created encrypted volume to an instance:

```
openstack server add volume <instance_id_or_name>
gitforgits-encrypted-db-volume
```

This attaches the encrypted volume to the specified instance, ready for use.

Verifying Volume Encryption

After creating and attaching the encrypted volume, it's important to verify that the encryption is active.

- SSH into the Instance

Access the instance where the encrypted volume is attached:

```
ssh -i ~/.ssh/gitforgits-key ubuntu@<instance_ip>
```

- List Block Devices

List the block devices to verify that the encrypted volume is recognized:

```
lsblk
```

The output should show the encrypted volume as a block device, typically with the name **/dev/dm-0** or similar.

- Check Encryption Details

To ensure that the volume is encrypted, you can check the encryption details using the following command:

```
sudo cryptsetup status <device_name>
```

Replace **<device_name>** with the name of the encrypted block device (e.g., **/dev/dm-0**). The output should confirm that the device is encrypted with the specified cipher and key size.

Automating the Creation of Encrypted Volumes

To streamline the deployment of encrypted volumes, you can automate their creation using a script as below:

```
nano create_encrypted_volumes.sh
```

Add the following content to the script:

```bash
#!/bin/bash


# Variables

VOLUME_SIZE=50  # Size of each volume in GB

VOLUME_COUNT=3  # Number of volumes to create

VOLUME_TYPE="gitforgits-encrypted-volumes"

BASE_VOLUME_NAME="gitforgits-encrypted-volume"


# Loop to create multiple encrypted volumes

for i in $(seq 1 $VOLUME_COUNT); do

    VOLUME_NAME="${BASE_VOLUME_NAME}-${i}"
```

```
    openstack volume create --type $VOLUME_TYPE --size
$VOLUME_SIZE --description "Automated Encrypted Volume $i
for GitforGits" $VOLUME_NAME

    echo "Created encrypted volume $VOLUME_NAME"

done
```

This script creates three 50 GB encrypted volumes.

```
./create_encrypted_volumes.sh
```

The script will create the specified number of encrypted volumes and output their creation status.

In this recipe, we demonstrated how to implement volume encryption in Cinder using the Barbican key manager and Cinder CLI. We covered the steps to configure encryption for volumes, create encrypted volumes, attach them to instances, and verify the encryption status. Additionally, we provided a method for automating the creation of encrypted volumes so as to secure its data effectively and efficiently in the cloud environment.

Summary

To summarize, this chapter focused on managing block storage with Cinder and practical applications in the GitforGits environment. The chapter began by going over the process of creating and attaching volumes to instances, which allowed for persistent storage that could be used by the virtual machines deployed in the environment. This was followed by learning how to manage volume snapshots, which are critical for data protection because they capture the volume's state at a specific point in time and provide a method for quick restoration if necessary.

The chapter also covered backup and restore operations, followed by a deeper layer of data protection to ensure that data is securely backed up and restored from external storage. A significant portion of the chapter was dedicated to configuring Cinder to use various storage backends, with a particular emphasis on integrating Ceph as the storage backend for GitforGits. This included installing Ceph, configuring Cinder to work with it, and ensuring that the storage infrastructure was optimized for performance and scalability.

Then we moved on to automation, which involved automating volume management tasks with Cinder CLI such as automating volume creation, attachment, detachment, and deletion, streamlining operations, and minimizing manual effort. Finally, the chapter covered implementing volume encryption to secure data at rest which included configuring encryption types, creating encrypted volumes, and verifying the encryption status. All of these lessons together provided an in-depth view of how to effectively manage, secure, and automate block storage in an OpenStack environment.

CHAPTER 7: LOAD BALANCING WITH OCTAVIA

Introduction

In this chapter, we will learn how to use Octavia, the native LBaaS solution for OpenStack, to set up and administer load balancing in an OpenStack environment. This chapter will walk you through the process of configuring and managing load balancers to improve the reliability and performance of cloud-based applications.

The chapter begins with installing and configuring Octavia, and then you'll learn how to create and manage load balancer pools to distribute incoming requests to backend servers. The chapter then delves into configuring load balancer listeners and virtual IP addresses (VIPs). You'll also look into SSL termination, which secures traffic between clients and the load balancer by offloading SSL processing. Finally, the chapter discusses integrating Octavia with Neutron networking to ensure seamless operation and connectivity within your OpenStack cloud. By the end of this chapter, you will have a firm grasp on how to implement and manage load balancing to improve the availability and resilience of your applications.

Recipe 1: Installing and Configuring Octavia

Load Balancer as a Service (LBaaS) and Octavia

In cloud computing, ensuring that applications remain highly available and responsive is critical. LBaaS is a key feature that helps achieve this by distributing incoming network traffic across multiple servers. By balancing the load, LBaaS prevents any single server from becoming overwhelmed, improving both the performance and availability of applications. In the context of OpenStack, Octavia is the native LBaaS solution designed to integrate seamlessly with the rest of the OpenStack ecosystem.

What is LBaaS?

LBaaS, or Load Balancer as a Service, allows cloud administrators and users to deploy load balancers without worrying about the underlying infrastructure. It automates the process of distributing network traffic to multiple backend servers, ensuring efficient resource usage and high availability. LBaaS is particularly useful in environments where applications need to scale dynamically in response to varying workloads.

Introducing Octavia

Octavia is the official OpenStack service designed to provide LBaaS functionality. It is an advanced and highly scalable load balancing solution that operates by managing a fleet of virtual machines, known as amphorae, which act as load balancers. Octavia's design is based on the concept of a "controller-worker" architecture, where the Octavia controller manages and orchestrates the creation, configuration, and maintenance of the amphorae, while the amphorae themselves handle the actual load balancing tasks. Octavia supports a wide range of load balancing algorithms and features, including SSL termination, L7 content switching, and health monitoring.

In this recipe, we will walk through the process of installing and configuring Octavia to enable LBaaS in your OpenStack environment.

Preparing Environment for Octavia

Before installing Octavia, ensure that your OpenStack environment is running fine with the necessary components like Neutron (networking) and Keystone (identity service) already configured. If not, refer to the chapter 2 and chapter 4 to get both of them configured and working.

- Install Required Dependencies

On the controller node, install the necessary dependencies for Octavia:

```
sudo apt-get update

sudo apt-get install -y octavia-api octavia-health-
manager octavia-housekeeping octavia-worker python3-
octaviaclient
```

This command installs the core Octavia services and the Octavia CLI client.

- Create the Octavia Service User

Next, create a user for Octavia in Keystone:

```
openstack user create --domain default --password
<password> octavia

openstack role add --project service --user octavia admin
```

This command creates the **octavia** user and grants it the necessary roles.

- Create the Octavia Service and Endpoints

Register the Octavia service in Keystone:

```
openstack service create --name octavia --description
"OpenStack Load Balancing" load-balancer
```

Create the API endpoints for Octavia:

```
openstack endpoint create --region RegionOne load-
balancer public http://<controller_ip>:9876

openstack endpoint create --region RegionOne load-
balancer internal http://<controller_ip>:9876

openstack endpoint create --region RegionOne load-
balancer admin http://<controller_ip>:9876
```

This command registers the Octavia service endpoints in Keystone, allowing it to be accessed by other OpenStack components.

Configuring Octavia

After the initial setup, you need to configure Octavia to integrate with the rest of your OpenStack environment.

Configure the Octavia API

Edit the Octavia configuration file **/etc/octavia/octavia.conf**:

```
sudo nano /etc/octavia/octavia.conf
```

In the **[DEFAULT]** section, configure the basics:

```
[DEFAULT]

transport_url =
rabbit://openstack:<RABBITMQ_PASSWORD>@<controller_ip>

auth_strategy = keystone
```

In the **[keystone_authtoken]** section, configure Keystone authentication:

```
[keystone_authtoken]

www_authenticate_uri = http://<controller_ip>:5000
```

```
auth_url = http://<controller_ip>:5000

memcached_servers = <controller_ip>:11211

auth_type = password

project_domain_name = Default

user_domain_name = Default

project_name = service

username = octavia

password = <password>
```

In the **[controller_worker]** section, configure the amphora image:

```
[controller_worker]

amp_image_tag = <amphora_image_tag>

amp_flavor_id = <flavor_id>

amp_boot_network_list = <network_id>
```

Here,

- **<amphora_image_tag>**: The tag or name of the amphora image used for load balancing.

- **<flavor_id>**: The ID of the flavor used for the amphora instances.

- **<network_id>**: The ID of the management network where amphorae will be deployed.

Configure the Amphora Image

Octavia uses amphorae, which are virtual machines running HAProxy, to perform load balancing. You need to create and upload an amphora image:

- Download the Amphora Image

```
wget https://tarballs.openstack.org/octavia/test-
images/test-only-amphora-x64-haproxy.qcow2
```

- Upload the Image to Glance

```
openstack image create "amphora-x64-haproxy" --file test-
only-amphora-x64-haproxy.qcow2 --disk-format qcow2 --
container-format bare --tag amphora
```

This command uploads the amphora image to Glance and tags it appropriately.

- Restart Octavia Services

Once the configuration is complete, restart the Octavia services to apply the changes:

```
sudo systemctl restart octavia-worker

sudo systemctl restart octavia-health-manager

sudo systemctl restart octavia-housekeeping

sudo systemctl restart octavia-api
```

Verifying Working of Octavia

Finally, verify that Octavia has been successfully installed and configured.

- Check the Service Status

Ensure that all Octavia services are running:

```
sudo systemctl status octavia-worker octavia-health-
manager octavia-housekeeping octavia-api
```

All services should show as active and running.

- Test the Octavia CLI

Use the Octavia CLI to ensure it's working correctly:

```
openstack loadbalancer list
```

Since you haven't created any load balancers yet, this command should return an empty list. However, it confirms that Octavia is correctly integrated with OpenStack.

In this recipe, we introduced the concept of LBaaS and provided a detailed overview of the Octavia component within OpenStack. We then walked through the process of installing and configuring Octavia, ensuring it's ready to provide load balancing services in the GitforGits environment.

Recipe 2: Creating and Managing Load Balancer Pools

In Octavia, a load balancer pool is a logical set of servers that share the incoming traffic. The load balancer distributes incoming requests across the members of the pool based on the selected load balancing algorithm. Managing load balancer pools effectively provides high availability, optimizing performance, and ensuring that your applications can handle varying loads. In this recipe, we'll walk through the process of creating load balancers for GitforGits, and then we'll explore how to manage these pools under different scenarios.

Creating a Load Balancer

The first step in setting up a load balancer is to create the load balancer itself, which will distribute traffic across the backend servers (pool members).

Create a Load Balancer

Use the following command to create a new load balancer:

```
openstack loadbalancer create --name gitforgits-lb --vip-
subnet-id <subnet_id>
```

Here,

- **--name gitforgits-lb**: The name of the load balancer.

- **--vip-subnet-id <subnet_id>**: The subnet ID where the VIP of the load balancer will be created.

This command creates a load balancer named **gitforgits-lb** with a virtual IP in the specified subnet.

Check Load Balancer Status

After creating the load balancer, check its status:

```
openstack loadbalancer show gitforgits-lb
```

The status should initially show as **PENDING_CREATE** and then change to **ACTIVE** once the load balancer is ready.

Creating and Managing Load Balancer Pools

Once the load balancer is created, the next step is to set up the pool that will distribute traffic among the backend servers.

Create a Load Balancer Pool

Create a pool for the load balancer:

```
openstack loadbalancer pool create --name gitforgits-pool
--lb-algorithm ROUND_ROBIN --listener <listener_id> --
protocol HTTP
```

Here,

- **--name gitforgits-pool**: The name of the pool.

- **--lb-algorithm ROUND_ROBIN**: The load balancing algorithm to use (e.g., ROUND_ROBIN, LEAST_CONNECTIONS, SOURCE_IP).

- **--listener <listener_id>**: The ID of the listener that the pool will use.

- **--protocol HTTP**: The protocol used by the pool.

Replace **<listener_id>** with the ID of the listener associated with the load balancer. This command creates a pool named **gitforgits-pool** that uses the ROUND_ROBIN algorithm to distribute HTTP traffic.

Add Members to the Pool

Once the pool is created, add members (backend servers) to the pool:

```
openstack loadbalancer member create --subnet-id
<subnet_id> --address <server_ip> --protocol-port 80
gitforgits-pool
```

Repeat this command for each server you want to add to the pool. For example:

```
openstack loadbalancer member create --subnet-id
<subnet_id> --address 192.168.1.10 --protocol-port 80
gitforgits-pool

openstack loadbalancer member create --subnet-id
<subnet_id> --address 192.168.1.11 --protocol-port 80
gitforgits-pool
```

This adds two members to the **gitforgits-pool**, with IP addresses **192.168.1.10** and **192.168.1.11**.

Check Pool Status

After adding members, check the status of the pool:

```
openstack loadbalancer pool show gitforgits-pool
```

The status should indicate that the pool is **ACTIVE** and list the members that were added.

Managing Load Balancer Pools

Effective management of load balancer pools involves monitoring, scaling, and updating pools based on traffic patterns and application requirements.

Scenario 1: Scaling the Pool

As traffic increases, you may need to scale the pool by adding more backend servers:

```
openstack loadbalancer member create --subnet-id
<subnet_id> --address 192.168.1.12 --protocol-port 80
gitforgits-pool
```

This command adds a new member to the pool, allowing the load balancer to distribute traffic across an additional server.

If a server is underperforming or needs to be taken offline for maintenance, you can remove it from the pool:

```
openstack loadbalancer member delete gitforgits-pool
<member_id>
```

This command removes the specified member from the pool.

Scenario 2: Changing the Load Balancing Algorithm

Depending on the application's needs, you might need to change the load balancing algorithm:

```
openstack loadbalancer pool set --lb-algorithm
LEAST_CONNECTIONS gitforgits-pool
```

This command changes the load balancing algorithm for **gitforgits-pool** to **LEAST_CONNECTIONS**, which directs traffic to the server with the fewest active connections.

Scenario 3: Monitoring and Health Checking

Regular monitoring and health checking ensure that all pool members are performing optimally. Here, health monitors can be added to ensure that traffic is only sent to healthy servers:

```
openstack loadbalancer healthmonitor create --delay 5 --
timeout 3 --max-retries 3 --type HTTP --pool gitforgits-
pool --url-path /
```

In the above code,

- **--delay 5**: The time in seconds between health checks.
- **--timeout 3**: The time in seconds to wait for a response.
- **--max-retries 3**: The number of retries before marking a member as unhealthy.
- **--type HTTP**: The protocol used by the health monitor.
- **--url-path /**: The URL path to check.

This command creates a health monitor that checks each member of **gitforgits-pool** every 5 seconds. If a member fails to respond three times in a row, it is marked as unhealthy and removed from the pool until it recovers.

Then, verify the health monitor status:

```
openstack loadbalancer healthmonitor show
<healthmonitor_id>
```

This command provides the status and configuration details of the health monitor.

Testing and Verifying Load Balancer Functionality

After setting up and managing the load balancer pools, it's important to test the configuration to ensure everything is functioning as expected. For this, **access** the VIP of the load balancer to verify that traffic is correctly distributed among the pool members:

```
curl http://<vip_ip>
```

The response should indicate that the traffic is being handled by one of the backend servers. And, to test the robustness of the load balancer, simulate a failure by shutting down one of the backend servers:

```
sudo systemctl stop apache2
```

Then, access the VIP again to ensure that the load balancer routes traffic to the remaining healthy servers.

In this recipe, we walked through the process of creating and managing load balancer pools using Octavia. We started by creating a load balancer and its associated pool, added members to the pool, and explored various management tasks such as scaling the pool, changing the load balancing algorithm, and configuring health monitors.

Recipe 3: Configuring Load Balancer Listeners and VIPs

Load Balancer Listeners and VIPs

In the context of Octavia, listeners and Virtual IPs (VIPs) are essential components of a load balancer that determine how traffic is handled and routed to backend servers. While the load balancer itself is responsible for distributing traffic across pool members, listeners define how the load balancer listens for incoming connections, and VIPs serve as the endpoint for these connections.

- **Listeners**: A listener is configured on a specific protocol and port, and it is responsible for receiving incoming traffic on the load balancer. The listener defines the protocol (e.g., HTTP, HTTPS, TCP) and the port number on which the load balancer will accept traffic. Each listener is associated with a load balancer and directs traffic to the appropriate pool based on its configuration.

- **VIPs**: The VIP is the IP address that clients use to access the load balancer. When clients send traffic to the VIP, the load balancer's listener receives this traffic and processes it according to the configured rules and algorithms. The VIP is a key element because it abstracts the actual IP addresses of the backend servers, providing a single entry point for accessing the load-balanced service.

In this recipe, we will configure listeners and VIPs for the load balancers created for GitforGits. We will walk through the steps to set up these components and ensure they are properly configured to handle incoming traffic.

Configuring a Load Balancer Listener

The first step in handling traffic is to set up a listener that will receive incoming connections on a specific protocol and port.

- Create a Listener

Use the following command to create a listener for the **gitforgits-lb** load balancer:

```
openstack loadbalancer listener create --name gitforgits-
http-listener --protocol HTTP --protocol-port 80 --
loadbalancer gitforgits-lb
```

This command creates an HTTP listener named **gitforgits-http-listener** that listens on port 80 for the **gitforgits-lb** load balancer.

- Verify Listener Configuration

After creating the listener, verify its configuration:

```
openstack loadbalancer listener show gitforgits-http-
listener
```

The output should display the details of the listener, including its protocol, port, and status. The status should be **ACTIVE** if the listener was successfully created.

Configuring VIP

The VIP is the address through which the load balancer is accessed by clients. This IP address is automatically assigned when the load balancer is created, but it's important to ensure it's configured correctly and associated with the correct listener.

- View the Assigned VIP

To view the VIP assigned to the load balancer, use the following command:

```
openstack loadbalancer show gitforgits-lb
```

Look for the **vip_address** field in the output, which shows the IP address assigned to the load balancer. This is the address that clients will use to send traffic to the load balancer.

If you need to assign a specific static IP as the VIP instead of using the automatically assigned one, you can specify it when creating the load balancer:

```
openstack loadbalancer create --name gitforgits-lb --vip-
address <static_ip> --vip-subnet-id <subnet_id>
```

Replace **<static_ip>** with the desired static IP address and **<subnet_id>** with the ID of the subnet where the VIP will reside. This command ensures that the load balancer uses a specific IP address as its VIP.

- Verify VIP Configuration

Ensure that the VIP is functioning correctly by checking its details:

```
openstack loadbalancer show gitforgits-lb
```

Confirm that the VIP is listed and associated with the correct subnet and load balancer.

Managing and Updating Listeners and VIPs

In a dynamic cloud environment, you may need to update or manage listeners and VIPs to handle different traffic patterns or application requirements.

- Update a Listener

If you need to change the listener's configuration, such as its protocol or port, you can update it using the following command:

```
openstack loadbalancer listener set --protocol HTTPS --
protocol-port 443 gitforgits-http-listener
```

This command changes the protocol to HTTPS and the port to 443. You might use this if you need to switch from HTTP to HTTPS for secure communications.

- Add a New Listener to the Same Load Balancer

You can add multiple listeners to the same load balancer, each handling different protocols or ports. For example, to add an HTTPS listener:

```
openstack loadbalancer listener create --name gitforgits-
https-listener --protocol HTTPS --protocol-port 443 --
loadbalancer gitforgits-lb
```

This adds a second listener to the **gitforgits-lb** load balancer, allowing it to handle both HTTP and HTTPS traffic.

1. **Monitor VIP Usage**
2. Monitoring the traffic through the VIP is important to ensure that the load balancer is distributing traffic as expected. You can use external monitoring tools or OpenStack's telemetry services (like Ceilometer) to track the load balancer's performance.

Testing Configuration

After setting up the listeners and VIP, it's crucial to test the configuration to ensure that traffic is properly routed through the load balancer.

- Access the Load Balancer via VIP

Test access to the load balancer by using the VIP:

```
curl http://<vip_ip>
```

The response should indicate that the request has been routed through the load balancer and handled by one of the backend servers.

- Test Different Protocols

If you have multiple listeners (e.g., HTTP and HTTPS), test each protocol by accessing the VIP with the appropriate protocol:

```
curl -k https://<vip_ip>
```

The **-k** flag is used to bypass SSL verification for testing purposes. This command should return a response indicating that the HTTPS listener is correctly routing traffic.

In this recipe, we started by creating and configuring listeners to handle incoming traffic on specific protocols and ports, and then we ensured that the VIP was correctly assigned and functional. And, we also covered managing and updating listeners and VIPs, allowing for flexibility in handling different traffic requirements.

Recipe 4: Using SSL Termination with Octavia

SSL Termination Overview

SSL termination is a process in which the SSL encryption and decryption tasks are offloaded from the backend servers to the load balancer. This means that incoming SSL-encrypted traffic is decrypted at the load balancer before being forwarded to the backend servers, and outgoing traffic is encrypted by the load balancer before being sent to the client. This approach reduces the computational load on backend servers, allowing them to focus on processing requests rather than handling encryption.

In the context of Octavia, SSL termination is an essential feature for securing communication between clients and the load balancer. By implementing SSL termination, you can ensure that data is encrypted as it traverses the internet, providing an additional layer of security for your applications. SSL termination also simplifies certificate management since the certificates are only required on the load balancer rather than on each backend server.

Preparing SSL Certificates

Before configuring SSL termination, you need to have SSL certificates ready. These certificates will be used by the load balancer to decrypt incoming SSL traffic.

- Generate a Self-Signed Certificate

For testing, you can generate a self-signed certificate using OpenSSL:

```
openssl req -x509 -newkey rsa:4096 -keyout octavia.key -out octavia.crt -days 365 -nodes
```

This command generates a private key (**octavia.key**) and a self-signed certificate (**octavia.crt**) that is valid for 365 days.

During the generation process, you will be prompted to enter information such as the country, state, and common name (CN). The CN should match the domain name that clients will use to access the load balancer.

- Create a Certificate Bundle

Octavia requires the private key and certificate to be combined into a single file, called a PEM (Privacy Enhanced Mail) file:

```
cat octavia.crt octavia.key > octavia.pem
```

This command creates a PEM file (**octavia.pem**) containing both the certificate and the private key.

Configuring SSL Termination on a Listener

With the certificate prepared, the next step is to configure SSL termination on an existing listener in Octavia.

- Create an HTTPS Listener with SSL Termination

Use the following command to create a listener that uses SSL termination:

```
openstack loadbalancer listener create --name gitforgits-
https-listener --protocol HTTPS --protocol-port 443 --
loadbalancer gitforgits-lb --default-tls-container-ref
<container_ref>
```

Replace **<container_ref>** with the actual reference to the container where the SSL certificate is stored. If you are using Barbican, OpenStack's secret storage service, you would first upload the PEM file to Barbican and use its container reference here.

Below is a quick example for uploading to Barbican:

```
openstack secret store --name octavia-cert --payload-
content-type='application/octet-stream' --payload="$(cat
octavia.pem)" --secret-type='certificate'
```

Then, retrieve the container reference:

```
openstack secret container create --name octavia-cert-
container --secret octavia-cert
```

Use the output from the above command as the **container_ref** when creating the listener.

- Verify the Listener Configuration

After creating the HTTPS listener with SSL termination, verify the configuration:

```
openstack loadbalancer listener show gitforgits-https-
listener
```

Check that the listener is configured to use the HTTPS protocol, is listening on port 443, and is associated with the correct TLS container.

Testing SSL Termination

Once the SSL termination is configured, it is needed to test it to ensure that it's working as expected.

- Access the Load Balancer via HTTPS

Use **curl** to test accessing the load balancer over HTTPS:

```
curl -k https://<vip_ip>
```

The response should indicate that the request has been routed through the load balancer and handled by one of the backend servers.

- Verify SSL Termination

To confirm that SSL termination is working correctly, inspect the traffic on the backend servers. Since SSL termination is handled by the load balancer, the traffic between the load balancer and the backend servers should be unencrypted HTTP.

Then, SSH into one of the backend servers and check the access logs:

```
sudo tail -f /var/log/apache2/access.log
```

The logs should show incoming HTTP requests from the load balancer, confirming that SSL was terminated at the load balancer and forwarded as HTTP to the backend.

Managing SSL Certificates

Managing SSL certificates is an ongoing task, especially in production environments where certificates need to be renewed and rotated regularly.

- Renewing Certificates

When it's time to renew the SSL certificate, generate a new certificate and upload it to Barbican as described earlier. Update the listener to use the new certificate:

```
openstack loadbalancer listener set --default-tls-
container-ref <new_container_ref> gitforgits-https-
listener
```

Replace **`<new_container_ref>`** with the reference to the new TLS container.

- Revoking Certificates

If a certificate is compromised, revoke it immediately and replace it with a new one. And then use the same process to update the listener with the new certificate.

Recipe 5: Integrating Octavia with Neutron Networking

Neutron provides connectivity as a service for other OpenStack services. Octavia relies heavily on Neutron to manage the network connectivity for load balancers, including the creation and management of VIPs, subnet attachments, and the routing of traffic to backend servers. Proper integration between Octavia and Neutron assures that load balancers can operate seamlessly within the existing network topology of your OpenStack environment.

In this recipe, we will focus on integrating Octavia with the existing Neutron setup in the GitforGits environment. This includes configuring the network resources that Octavia requires and ensuring that load balancers are correctly connected to the Neutron-managed networks.

Reviewing existing Neutron Network

Before integrating Octavia with Neutron, it's important to understand the existing network setup within Neutron. This will help in planning how the load balancers will interact with the networks and subnets already in use.

- List Existing Networks and Subnets

Begin by listing the existing networks and subnets in Neutron:

```
openstack network list

openstack subnet list
```

This command provides a list of all networks and subnets currently configured in Neutron. Identify the network that will be used for the load balancer's VIP and the networks to which the backend servers are connected.

- Review Network Configuration

Then, examine the details of the selected network and subnet to ensure they meet the requirements for load balancer integration:

```
openstack network show <network_id>
```

```
openstack subnet show <subnet_id>
```

Configuring the Management Network

Octavia requires a dedicated management network to communicate with the amphorae (the virtual machines that perform the load balancing). This network is used for health monitoring, control plane traffic, and other internal communications.

- Create a Management Network

If a management network does not already exist, create one:

```
openstack network create octavia-mgmt-net
```

This command creates a new network named **octavia-mgmt-net** for managing the Octavia amphorae.

- Create a Subnet for the Management Network

Next, create a subnet within the management network:

```
openstack subnet create --network octavia-mgmt-net --subnet-range 192.168.100.0/24 --gateway 192.168.100.1 octavia-mgmt-subnet
```

This command creates a subnet named **octavia-mgmt-subnet** within the **octavia-mgmt-net** network, with the specified IP range.

- Verify the Management Network Configuration

Confirm that the management network and subnet are correctly configured:

```
openstack network show octavia-mgmt-net
```

```
openstack subnet show octavia-mgmt-subnet
```

And then, ensure that the network and subnet are active and that the subnet configuration is correct.

Configuring Security Groups

Security groups in Neutron control the traffic allowed to and from instances, including the amphorae managed by Octavia. Proper security group configuration is essential to ensure that Octavia can communicate with the Neutron networks and perform its load balancing functions.

- Create a Security Group for Octavia

Create a dedicated security group for the Octavia management network:

```
openstack security group create octavia-mgmt-secgroup --
description "Security group for Octavia management
network"
```

This command creates a security group named **octavia-mgmt-secgroup**.

- Add Rules to the Security Group

Add the necessary rules to allow traffic between the Octavia services and the amphorae:

```
openstack security group rule create --protocol tcp --
dst-port 22:22 --remote-ip 192.168.100.0/24 octavia-mgmt-
secgroup

openstack security group rule create --protocol icmp
octavia-mgmt-secgroup

openstack security group rule create --protocol tcp --
dst-port 9443:9443 --remote-ip 192.168.100.0/24 octavia-
mgmt-secgroup
```

Here, the first rule allows SSH traffic on port 22. The second rule allows ICMP traffic (for ping). And, the third rule allows HTTPS traffic on port 9443, which is used for Octavia's API and management traffic.

- Associate the Security Group with the Management Network

Ensure that the security group is associated with the instances (amphorae) that Octavia manages. This is typically handled automatically during amphora creation, but you can manually verify and adjust as needed.

Configuring Neutron for Octavia Integration

With the management network and security groups in place, the next step is to configure Neutron to work seamlessly with Octavia.

- Edit Neutron Configuration

Update the Neutron configuration file (**/etc/neutron/neutron.conf**) to include settings specific to Octavia:

```
sudo nano /etc/neutron/neutron.conf
```

In the **[service_providers]** section, ensure Octavia is listed as the provider for LBaaS:

```
[service_providers]

service_provider=LOADBALANCER:Octavia:octavia_driver:defa
ult
```

This line specifies that Octavia is the default load balancer service provider.

- Restart Neutron Services

Restart the Neutron services to apply the configuration changes:

```
sudo systemctl restart neutron-server
```

This command restarts the Neutron server to ensure that the new configuration is loaded.

Deploying a Load Balancer with Neutron Integration

With Octavia and Neutron fully integrated, you can now deploy a load balancer and verify that it works within the Neutron-managed networks.

- Create a Load Balancer

Use the following command to create a new load balancer within a Neutron network:

```
openstack loadbalancer create --name gitforgits-lb --vip-
subnet-id <subnet_id>
```

Replace **<subnet_id>** with the ID of the subnet managed by Neutron where the VIP will be created. This command creates a load balancer named **gitforgits-lb**.

- Create a Listener

Create a listener for the load balancer:

```
openstack loadbalancer listener create --name gitforgits-
http-listener --protocol HTTP --protocol-port 80 --
loadbalancer gitforgits-lb
```

This creates an HTTP listener on port 80 for the load balancer.

- Create a Pool and Add Members

Create a pool and add backend servers to the load balancer:

```
openstack loadbalancer pool create --name gitforgits-pool
--lb-algorithm ROUND_ROBIN --listener gitforgits-http-
listener --protocol HTTP

openstack loadbalancer member create --subnet-id
<subnet_id> --address <server_ip> --protocol-port 80
gitforgits-pool
```

This command sets up a pool with a round-robin load balancing algorithm and adds members (backend servers) to it. And then verify that the load balancer is functioning correctly within the Neutron-managed network.

- Test Access to the Load Balancer

Use **curl** or a web browser to access the load balancer's VIP:

```
curl http://<vip_ip>
```

The response should indicate that traffic is being routed through the load balancer to one of the backend servers.

In this recipe, the integration has ensured load balancers can efficiently distribute traffic across backend servers while fully utilizing the networking capabilities provided by Neutron.

Summary

In conclusion, we acquired the ability to manage and implement load balancing with Octavia in order to improve the performance and reliability of applications. We initiated the process by installing and configuring Octavia as the LBaaS solution, ensuring that it was seamlessly integrated with the current OpenStack configuration. The chapter subsequently explored the creation and management of load balancer pools, which facilitate the efficient distribution of traffic among backend servers through the use of algorithms such as round-robin. This approach ensures high availability and load distribution.

In addition, we acquired the knowledge necessary to configure load balancer listeners and VIPs, which are essential for routing incoming traffic to the appropriate backend servers. The listeners were configured to manage traffic in a secure and accurate manner by accommodating various protocols and ports. We implemented SSL termination to offload encryption and decryption tasks from backend servers to the load balancer, thereby reducing the computational load on the servers and enhancing security.

Lastly, we ensured that Octavia operated seamlessly within the current network topology by integrating it with Neutron, OpenStack's networking component. As part of the integration, a dedicated management network was configured, security groups were set up, and the ability of load balancers to function properly within the networks managed by Neutron was verified.

CHAPTER 8:
ORCHESTRATION WITH HEAT

Introduction

Until now, we have explored OpenStack's compute, storage, networking, and load balancing components in the previous chapters, giving GitforGits the tools it needs to manage a robust cloud infrastructure. We have acquired the ability to deploy and manage virtual machines, secure data with encrypted storage, balance network traffic using Octavia, and seamlessly integrate these components within a dynamic cloud environment. Starting with this foundation, in this chapter, we will now concentrate on orchestration through the use of Heat, the native orchestration service of OpenStack.

In the final chapter of this book, we will explore the automation and management of complex cloud environments using Heat, which enables Infrastructure as Code (IaC). The chapter commences with the installation and configuration of Heat, which guarantees that your environment is prepared for orchestration. We subsequently proceed to the development and deployment of Heat templates, which facilitate the effective management of stacks, resources, and dependencies within your cloud.

Furthermore, we will investigate the possibility of integrating auto-scaling with Heat and Ceilometer to dynamically adjust resources in accordance with demand, thereby achieving optimal performance and cost efficiency. We will acquire the ability to employ Heat for Infrastructure as Code for the purpose of versioning, testing, and deploying infrastructure configurations in a repeatable manner. Finally, we will resolve common troubleshooting issues in Heat orchestration to guarantee the smooth and dependable operation of your cloud environment.

Recipe 1: Installing and Configuring Heat for Orchestration

Introduction to Heat and Orchestration

Heat is the orchestration component of OpenStack, designed to automate the deployment and management of cloud resources. Orchestration refers to the automated arrangement, coordination, and management of complex computer systems, middleware, and services. Heat provides a way to manage cloud applications and resources using templates that define the infrastructure as code (IaC). These templates, written in YAML or JSON, define the infrastructure resources that need to be deployed, such as instances, floating IPs, volumes, security groups, and more. The key advantage of Heat is its ability to manage the entire lifecycle of an application, from initial deployment to updates and scaling operations.

Heat's orchestration capabilities make it possible to define an entire cloud environment as code, enabling Infrastructure as Code (IaC) practices. This allows for versioning, testing, and deployment of infrastructure in a consistent and controlled manner. With Heat, GitforGits can automate the creation and management of complex environments, reducing the manual effort required to deploy and scale resources.

Installing Heat

Before using Heat, it must be installed and configured in your existing OpenStack environment. This involves setting up the Heat service components and ensuring they are integrated with other OpenStack services as per the given below steps:

- Install Heat Packages

On the controller node, install the Heat packages:

```
sudo apt-get update

sudo apt-get install -y heat-api heat-api-cfn heat-engine
python3-heatclient
```

This command installs the core Heat services: **heat-api**, **heat-api-cfn** (which provides AWS CloudFormation-compatible APIs), and **heat-engine**, as well as the **python3-heatclient** CLI tool for interacting with Heat.

- Create the Heat Database

Next, create a database for Heat:

```
mysql -u root -p
```

In the MySQL prompt, run the following commands:

```
CREATE DATABASE heat;

GRANT ALL PRIVILEGES ON heat.* TO 'heat'@'localhost'
IDENTIFIED BY '<password>';

GRANT ALL PRIVILEGES ON heat.* TO 'heat'@'%' IDENTIFIED
BY '<password>';

FLUSH PRIVILEGES;

EXIT;
```

- Configure Heat to use Database

Edit the Heat configuration file to use the newly created database:

```
sudo nano /etc/heat/heat.conf
```

In the **[database]** section, add the following:

```
[database]

connection =
mysql+pymysql://heat:<password>@localhost/heat
```

- Register Heat in Keystone

```
openstack user create --domain default --password
<password> heat

openstack role add --project service --user heat admin

openstack service create --name heat --description
"Orchestration" orchestration

openstack service create --name heat-cfn --description
"Orchestration" cloudformation
```

- Create Heat Endpoints

Create the API endpoints for Heat:

```
openstack endpoint create --region RegionOne
orchestration public
http://<controller_ip>:8004/v1/%\(tenant_id\)s

openstack endpoint create --region RegionOne
orchestration internal
http://<controller_ip>:8004/v1/%\(tenant_id\)s
```

```
openstack endpoint create --region RegionOne
orchestration admin
http://<controller_ip>:8004/v1/%\(tenant_id\)s

openstack endpoint create --region RegionOne
cloudformation public http://<controller_ip>:8000/v1

openstack endpoint create --region RegionOne
cloudformation internal http://<controller_ip>:8000/v1

openstack endpoint create --region RegionOne
cloudformation admin http://<controller_ip>:8000/v1
```

These above huge list of commands register the Heat service and CloudFormation-compatible endpoints in Keystone.

- Configure Heat Services

In the Heat configuration file (**/etc/heat/heat.conf**), set the Keystone authentication details:

```
[keystone_authtoken]

www_authenticate_uri = http://<controller_ip>:5000

auth_url = http://<controller_ip>:5000

memcached_servers = <controller_ip>:11211

auth_type = password

project_domain_name = Default

user_domain_name = Default

project_name = service

username = heat

password = <password>
```

- Populate the Heat Database

Initialize the Heat database:

```
sudo heat-manage db_sync
```

This command populates the database with the necessary tables and data. And then finally, start the Heat services and enable them to start at boot:

```
sudo systemctl enable heat-api heat-api-cfn heat-engine

sudo systemctl start heat-api heat-api-cfn heat-engine

sudo systemctl status heat-api heat-api-cfn heat-engine
```

All services should be active and running.

With this, Heat is fully operational and ready to be used for orchestrating complex cloud environments. This Heat can streamline our infrastructure management, automate deployment processes, and adopt Infrastructure as Code practices, ultimately leading to a more efficient and scalable cloud environment.

Recipe 2: Creating and Deploying Heat Templates for Stack Management

In this recipe, we will walk through the process of creating and deploying a Heat template to manage a stack within the GitforGits environment. The Heat template will define the infrastructure resources that are required, and then we will deploy it as a stack to automate the provisioning and management of these resources.

Creating a Heat Template

Define the Heat Template

First, create a new YAML file to define the Heat template. This template will include resources such as a virtual machine, a security group, and a floating IP.

- Create the template file:

```
nano gitforgits-heat-template.yaml
```

- Add the following content to the file:

```
heat_template_version: 2018-08-31

description: >

  Heat template to deploy a simple stack for GitforGits.

parameters:

  image_id:

    type: string

    description: ID of the image to use for the instance.

  instance_type:

    type: string

    description: Flavor to use for the instance.

    default: m1.small

  network_id:

    type: string

    description: Network ID to attach the instance to.

resources:

  gitforgits_security_group:

    type: OS::Neutron::SecurityGroup
```

```yaml
  properties:
    description: Security group for GitforGits instance
    rules:
      - protocol: tcp
        port_range_min: 22
        port_range_max: 22
        remote_ip_prefix: 0.0.0.0/0


gitforgits_instance:
  type: OS::Nova::Server
  properties:
    name: gitforgits-instance
    image: { get_param: image_id }
    flavor: { get_param: instance_type }
    networks:
      - network: { get_param: network_id }
    security_groups: [gitforgits_security_group]

gitforgits_floating_ip:
  type: OS::Neutron::FloatingIP
  properties:
```

```
      floating_network: public

      port_id: { get_resource: gitforgits_instance }


outputs:

  instance_ip:

    description: The IP address of the GitforGits
instance

    value: { get_attr: [gitforgits_floating_ip,
floating_ip_address] }
```

This template defines:

- A security group that allows SSH access.

- A Nova instance (**gitforgits_instance**) that will be created using the specified image and flavor.

- A floating IP that will be associated with the instance.

Deploying the Heat Template as a Stack

Deploy the Stack

Use the **openstack** CLI to deploy the Heat template as a stack:

```
openstack stack create -t gitforgits-heat-template.yaml -
-parameter image_id=<image_id> --parameter
network_id=<network_id> GitforGits-Stack
```

Here,

- **-t gitforgits-heat-template.yaml**: Specifies the path to the Heat template file.

- **--parameter image_id=<image_id>**: Passes the ID of the image to use for the instance.

- **`--parameter network_id=<network_id>`**: Passes the network ID to which the instance should be attached.

Verify the Stack Deployment

Once the stack is deployed, verify that the resources have been created:

```
openstack stack show GitforGits-Stack
```

This command displays details about the stack, including the outputs such as the floating IP address of the instance.

And then, SSH into the instance using the floating IP provided in the stack output:

```
ssh -i ~/.ssh/gitforgits-key ubuntu@<floating_ip>
```

In this recipe, we demonstrated how to create and deploy a Heat template to manage a stack in the GitforGits environment. By using Heat templates for stack management, one can automate the deployment of complex environments and reduce the manual effort required to manage cloud resources.

Recipe 3: Implementing Auto-Scaling with Heat and Ceilometer

Auto-Scaling and Its Advantages

Auto-scaling is a powerful feature in cloud environments that automatically adjusts the number of active instances or resources based on the current demand. This capability maintains the performance and cost-efficiency of applications. For GitforGits, auto-scaling ensures that the infrastructure can dynamically adapt to changes in workload, scaling out resources during peak times and scaling in during periods of low demand. This not only optimizes resource utilization but also reduces costs by ensuring that only the necessary resources are running at any given time.

Auto-scaling is typically implemented using Heat templates combined with telemetry data provided by Ceilometer. Heat orchestrates the creation, update, and deletion of resources, while Ceilometer monitors and collects data about resource usage, triggering scaling actions based on predefined criteria.

Up and Running with Ceilometer

What is Ceilometer?

Ceilometer is the telemetry service responsible for collecting and providing data on the utilization of resources within an OpenStack cloud. It enables monitoring and metering, allowing administrators to track usage patterns, generate billing data, and trigger events such as auto-scaling. Ceilometer collects data from various OpenStack services, including Nova, Cinder, Neutron, and Swift, and stores it for analysis and action.

For GitforGits, Ceilometer will be used to monitor the usage of compute resources (e.g., CPU utilization) and trigger auto-scaling events through Heat when certain thresholds are met.

Installing Ceilometer

- Install Ceilometer Packages

On the controller node, install the Ceilometer packages:

```
sudo apt-get update

sudo apt-get install -y ceilometer-api ceilometer-collector ceilometer-agent-central ceilometer-agent-notification python3-ceilometerclient
```

This command installs the core Ceilometer services, including the API, collector, and agents.

Configure Ceilometer to Use MongoDB

Ceilometer requires a database to store the collected telemetry data. MongoDB is commonly used for this purpose.

- Install MongoDB

```
sudo apt-get install -y mongodb-server
```

Configure Ceilometer to use MongoDB by editing the **/etc/ceilometer/ceilometer.conf** file:

```
sudo nano /etc/ceilometer/ceilometer.conf
```

In the **[database]** section, add the following:

```
[database]

connection = mongodb://localhost:27017/ceilometer
```

This configuration connects Ceilometer to a local MongoDB instance.

Create Ceilometer Database and User

Create the Ceilometer database and user in MongoDB:

```
mongo --host localhost --eval 'db =
db.getSiblingDB("ceilometer"); db.createUser({user:
"ceilometer", pwd: "<password>", roles: [ "readWrite",
"dbAdmin" ]})'
```

Create the Ceilometer Service and Endpoints

Register Ceilometer in Keystone:

```
openstack user create --domain default --password
<password> ceilometer

openstack role add --project service --user ceilometer
admin

openstack service create --name ceilometer --description
"Telemetry" metering
```

Create the API endpoints for Ceilometer:

```
openstack endpoint create --region RegionOne metering
public http://<controller_ip>:8777

openstack endpoint create --region RegionOne metering
internal http://<controller_ip>:8777

openstack endpoint create --region RegionOne metering
admin http://<controller_ip>:8777
```

Start and Enable Ceilometer Services

Start the Ceilometer services and enable them to start at boot:

```
sudo systemctl enable ceilometer-api ceilometer-collector
ceilometer-agent-central ceilometer-agent-notification

sudo systemctl start ceilometer-api ceilometer-collector
ceilometer-agent-central ceilometer-agent-notification
```

Verify that the services are running:

```
sudo systemctl status ceilometer-api ceilometer-collector
ceilometer-agent-central ceilometer-agent-notification
```

All services should be active and running.

Implementing Auto-Scaling with Heat and Ceilometer

With Ceilometer installed and collecting data, we can now set up auto-scaling using Heat templates. This involves creating a Heat template that defines the auto-scaling group, specifying scaling policies, and integrating Ceilometer metrics to trigger scaling actions.

Creating the Heat Template for Auto-Scaling

Create a new YAML file for the Heat template:

```
nano gitforgits-autoscaling-template.yaml
```

Add the following content to the file:

```
heat_template_version: 2018-08-31


description: >

  Heat template to deploy an auto-scaling group for
GitforGits.


parameters:
```

```yaml
  image_id:

    type: string

    description: ID of the image to use for the
instances.

  instance_type:

    type: string

    description: Flavor to use for the instances.

    default: m1.small

  network_id:

    type: string

    description: Network ID to attach the instances to.


resources:

  gitforgits_scaling_group:

    type: OS::Heat::AutoScalingGroup

    properties:

      min_size: 1

      max_size: 5

      desired_capacity: 2

      resource:

        type: OS::Nova::Server

        properties:
```

```yaml
        image: { get_param: image_id }

        flavor: { get_param: instance_type }

        networks:

            - network: { get_param: network_id }


  cpu_alarm_high:

    type: OS::Ceilometer::Alarm

    properties:

        description: Scale-up if CPU > 70% for 1 minute

        meter_name: cpu_util

        statistic: avg

        period: 60

        evaluation_periods: 1

        threshold: 70

        comparison_operator: gt

        alarm_actions:

          - { get_attr: [scale_up_policy, alarm_url] }

        matching_metadata: {'metadata.user_metadata.stack':
{get_param: "OS::stack_name"}}


  cpu_alarm_low:
```

```
    type: OS::Ceilometer::Alarm

    properties:

      description: Scale-down if CPU < 30% for 1 minute

      meter_name: cpu_util

      statistic: avg

      period: 60

      evaluation_periods: 1

      threshold: 30

      comparison_operator: lt

      alarm_actions:

        - { get_attr: [scale_down_policy, alarm_url] }

      matching_metadata: {'metadata.user_metadata.stack':
{get_param: "OS::stack_name"}}


  scale_up_policy:

    type: OS::Heat::ScalingPolicy

    properties:

      adjustment_type: change_in_capacity

      scaling_adjustment: 1

      auto_scaling_group_id: { get_resource:
gitforgits_scaling_group }
```

```
scale_down_policy:

  type: OS::Heat::ScalingPolicy

  properties:

    adjustment_type: change_in_capacity

    scaling_adjustment: -1

    auto_scaling_group_id: { get_resource:
gitforgits_scaling_group }


outputs:

  autoscaling_group:

    description: The ID of the auto-scaling group

    value: { get_resource: gitforgits_scaling_group }
```

This template defines:

- An auto-scaling group (**gitforgits_scaling_group**) that can scale between 1 and 5 instances.

- Ceilometer alarms (**cpu_alarm_high** and **cpu_alarm_low**) to trigger scaling actions based on CPU utilization.

- Scaling policies (**scale_up_policy** and **scale_down_policy**) to adjust the number of instances based on the alarms.

Deploy and Monitor Auto-Scaling Stack

Use the **openstack** CLI to deploy the auto-scaling stack:

```
openstack stack create -t gitforgits-autoscaling-
template.yaml --parameter image_id=<image_id> --parameter
network_id=<network_id> GitforGits-AutoScaling
```

After deploying the stack, monitor the status of the auto-scaling group:

```
openstack stack show GitforGits-AutoScaling
```

This command displays details about the stack, including the current number of instances in the auto-scaling group.

Testing and Verifying Auto-Scaling

SSH into one of the instances in the auto-scaling group and simulate a high CPU load to trigger the scaling-up action:

```
stress --cpu 8 --timeout 300
```

This command generates CPU load for 5 minutes. Ceilometer should detect the high CPU usage and trigger the **cpu_alarm_high**, causing Heat to scale up the number of instances.

Later, use the following command to verify that additional instances have been launched:

```
openstack stack resource list GitforGits-AutoScaling
```

This command lists the resources in the stack, showing the updated number of instances. After the high load period, the CPU usage should drop. Ceilometer will detect this and trigger the **cpu_alarm_low**, causing Heat to scale down the number of instances.

Now, check that the number of instances has decreased:

```
openstack stack resource list GitforGits-AutoScaling
```

The resource list should show fewer instances in the auto-scaling group.

In this recipe, we started by installing Ceilometer, which collects and monitors telemetry data necessary for triggering scaling actions. We then created a Heat template to define an auto-scaling group, with Ceilometer alarms set to adjust the number of instances based on CPU utilization. Finally, we deployed the stack and verified the auto-scaling functionality by simulating high and low CPU loads, ensuring that the number of instances dynamically adjusted to match the workload.

Recipe 4: Using Heat for Infrastructure as Code (IaC)

Infrastructure as Code (IaC) is a practice that allows infrastructure to be managed and provisioned through code rather than manual processes. This approach brings the benefits of version control, consistency, automation, and collaboration to infrastructure management, much like traditional software development. Heat, as an orchestration tool, is well-suited for implementing IaC by using templates to define and automate the deployment and management of cloud resources.

Here in this recipe, we will demonstrate how to use Heat to perform IaC tasks for the GitforGits infrastructure. This involves creating a Heat template that defines the entire infrastructure, including compute, networking, and storage resources, and then deploying this template to manage the infrastructure as code.

Defining Heat Template for IaC

Start by creating a new YAML file that defines the complete infrastructure for GitforGits:

```
nano gitforgits-iac-template.yaml
```

Then, add the following content to the file:

```
heat_template_version: 2018-08-31


description: >

  Heat template for Infrastructure as Code (IaC)
deployment for GitforGits.


parameters:
  image_id:
    type: string
    description: ID of the image to use for the
instances.
  instance_type:
    type: string
```

```yaml
    description: Flavor to use for the instances.

    default: m1.small
  network_id:

    type: string

    description: Network ID to attach the instances to.
  key_name:

    type: string

    description: Name of the SSH key pair to access
instances.


resources:
  gitforgits_network:

    type: OS::Neutron::Net

    properties:

      name: gitforgits-network


  gitforgits_subnet:

    type: OS::Neutron::Subnet

    properties:

      network_id: { get_resource: gitforgits_network }

      cidr: 192.168.10.0/24

      ip_version: 4
```

```yaml
      gateway_ip: 192.168.10.1


  gitforgits_router:

    type: OS::Neutron::Router

    properties:

      name: gitforgits-router

      external_gateway_info:

        network: public


  gitforgits_router_interface:

    type: OS::Neutron::RouterInterface

    properties:

      router_id: { get_resource: gitforgits_router }

      subnet_id: { get_resource: gitforgits_subnet }


  gitforgits_security_group:

    type: OS::Neutron::SecurityGroup

    properties:

      description: Security group for GitforGits
instances

      rules:

        - protocol: tcp
```

```
            port_range_min: 22

            port_range_max: 22

            remote_ip_prefix: 0.0.0.0/0

          - protocol: tcp

            port_range_min: 80

            port_range_max: 80

            remote_ip_prefix: 0.0.0.0/0


gitforgits_instance_1:

  type: OS::Nova::Server

  properties:

    name: gitforgits-instance-1

    image: { get_param: image_id }

    flavor: { get_param: instance_type }

    key_name: { get_param: key_name }

    networks:

      - network: { get_resource: gitforgits_network }

    security_groups: [gitforgits_security_group]


gitforgits_instance_2:

  type: OS::Nova::Server
```

```yaml
  properties:

    name: gitforgits-instance-2

    image: { get_param: image_id }

    flavor: { get_param: instance_type }

    key_name: { get_param: key_name }

    networks:

      - network: { get_resource: gitforgits_network }

    security_groups: [gitforgits_security_group]


gitforgits_volume:

  type: OS::Cinder::Volume

  properties:

    size: 10

    name: gitforgits-volume


gitforgits_volume_attachment:

  type: OS::Cinder::VolumeAttachment

  properties:

    instance_uuid: { get_resource:
gitforgits_instance_1 }

    volume_id: { get_resource: gitforgits_volume }

    mountpoint: /dev/vdb
```

```
outputs:

  instance_1_ip:

    description: The IP address of GitforGits instance 1

    value: { get_attr: [gitforgits_instance_1,
first_address] }

  instance_2_ip:

    description: The IP address of GitforGits instance 2

    value: { get_attr: [gitforgits_instance_2,
first_address] }

  volume_id:

    description: The ID of the GitforGits volume

    value: { get_resource: gitforgits_volume }
```

This template defines the entire infrastructure, including:

- A Neutron network and subnet.
- A router and interface to connect the subnet to the public network.
- A security group allowing SSH and HTTP traffic.
- Two Nova instances, each attached to the network and secured by the security group.
- A Cinder volume attached to one of the instances.

Deploying the Infrastructure as a Stack

Use the **openstack** CLI to deploy the Heat template as a stack:

```
openstack stack create -t gitforgits-iac-template.yaml --
parameter image_id=<image_id> --parameter
network_id=<network_id> --parameter key_name=<key_name>
GitforGits-IaC
```

Here,

- **-t gitforgits-iac-template.yaml**: Specifies the path to the Heat template file.
- **--parameter image_id=<image_id>**: Passes the ID of the image to use for the instances.
- **--parameter network_id=<network_id>**: Passes the network ID to which the instances should be attached.
- **--parameter key_name=<key_name>**: Passes the name of the SSH key pair for accessing the instances.
- **GitforGits-IaC**: The name of the stack to be created.

Next, monitor the status of the stack creation:

```
openstack stack list
```

The status will show as **CREATE_IN_PROGRESS** initially and will change to **CREATE_COMPLETE** once the stack is fully deployed.

Once the stack is deployed, verify that the resources have been created:

```
openstack stack show GitforGits-IaC
```

This command displays details about the stack, including the outputs such as the IP addresses of the instances and the ID of the attached volume.

Managing Infrastructure with Heat

If you need to make changes to the infrastructure, such as adding more instances or modifying the security group rules, update the template file and then update the stack:

```
openstack stack update -t gitforgits-iac-template.yaml
GitforGits-IaC
```

This command updates the stack with the new configuration, ensuring that the infrastructure is modified according to the updated template. Also, if you need to scale the infrastructure, such as adding more instances, modify the Heat template to include additional **OS::Nova::Server** resources, then update the stack:

```
gitforgits_instance_3:

  type: OS::Nova::Server

  properties:

    name: gitforgits-instance-3

    image: { get_param: image_id }

    flavor: { get_param: instance_type }

    key_name: { get_param: key_name }

    networks:

      - network: { get_resource: gitforgits_network }

    security_groups: [gitforgits_security_group]
```

Add this to the template, save, and then run the stack update command as before.

Recipe 5: Troubleshooting Heat Orchestration Issues

As the final recipe in this chapter and the book, we focus on troubleshooting common issues that may arise when using Heat for orchestration tasks in the GitforGits environment. While Heat is a powerful tool for managing infrastructure as code, various challenges can occur during the deployment, scaling, and management of resources. This recipe will address these potential issues and provide strategies for resolving them effectively.

Issue 1: Stack Creation Failures

The stack creation process fails with a **CREATE_FAILED** status.

Possible Causes

- Incorrect parameters or missing values in the Heat template.
- Insufficient resources available in the OpenStack environment (e.g., no available compute capacity, insufficient storage).
- Network issues preventing communication between the Heat engine and other OpenStack services.

Troubleshooting Steps

- Use the **openstack** CLI to examine the events associated with the stack:

```
openstack stack event list <stack_name>
```

Examine the status of individual resources to pinpoint the failure:

```
openstack stack resource list <stack_name>
```

Look for resources with a **CREATE_FAILED** status and use the resource ID to investigate further:

```
openstack stack resource show <stack_name> <resource_id>
```

Ensure that all required parameters are provided and correct. Check for typos, incorrect IDs, or missing values in the template.

Verify that there are sufficient resources in the environment. For example, check if there is enough available compute capacity, storage, or networking resources to fulfill the request.

Ensure that the Heat engine can communicate with other OpenStack services. Verify that the necessary ports are open and that no network segmentation issues are preventing communication.

Issue 2: Stack Update Failures

The stack update process fails, leaving the stack in a **ROLLBACK_IN_PROGRESS** or **UPDATE_FAILED** state.

Possible Causes

- Conflicts between existing resources and the updated template.

- Incomplete or incorrect update operations (e.g., trying to delete a resource that is still in use).

- Resource dependencies that prevent successful updates.

Troubleshooting Steps

- As with stack creation, use the **openstack** CLI to view the events related to the update:

```
openstack stack event list <stack_name>
```

Review the events to understand which resources caused the update to fail.

If the update failed due to a resource conflict (e.g., trying to delete a resource that is still in use), adjust the template to resolve the conflict. Ensure that dependencies are correctly handled in the template.

If your stack involves multiple instances, consider using a rolling update strategy to minimize disruption and reduce the chance of failure:

```
openstack stack update --rollback <stack_name>
```

This command ensures that the stack rolls back to the previous state if the update fails.

Review the template for resource dependencies. Ensure that resources are updated in the correct order, and that dependent resources are not prematurely modified or deleted.

Issue 3: Resource Deletion Failures

The stack deletion process fails, leaving the stack in a **DELETE_FAILED** state.

Possible Causes

- Resources that cannot be deleted due to ongoing dependencies or locks (e.g., volumes still attached to instances).

- Network or connectivity issues preventing the deletion of resources.

- Incomplete cleanup operations, such as dangling floating IPs or ports.

Troubleshooting Steps

- Use the **openstack** CLI to identify which resources failed to delete:

```
openstack stack resource list <stack_name>
```

Look for resources with a **DELETE_FAILED** status and use the resource ID to investigate further:

```
openstack stack resource show <stack_name> <resource_id>
```

Ensure that the resource is not still in use. For example, if a volume failed to delete, verify that it is no longer attached to any instances. Manually detach the volume if necessary:

```
openstack server remove volume <server_id> <volume_id>
```

If a resource is stuck, consider force-deleting it using the appropriate OpenStack service commands. For example, to force-delete a volume:

```
openstack volume delete --force <volume_id>
```

Repeat this process for other stuck resources as needed.

After resolving the issues, manually delete the stack:

```
openstack stack delete <stack_name>
```

Ensure that all associated resources are properly cleaned up.

Issue 4: Heat Template Validation Errors

The stack creation or update process fails with a template validation error.

Possible Causes

- Syntax errors or invalid resource definitions in the Heat template.
- Incorrect or unsupported template functions or resource types.

Troubleshooting Steps

- Before deploying or updating a stack, validate the template using the **heat-template-validate** command:

```
openstack orchestration template validate -t
<template_file>
```

This command checks the syntax and structure of the template to identify any issues before deployment.

Carefully review the error messages provided during validation. These messages often indicate the exact location and nature of the error.

Ensure that you are using supported resource types and functions. Refer to the official Heat documentation for a list of valid resources and their properties:

Fix any syntax errors or invalid resource definitions in the template. Common issues include incorrect indentation, missing parameters, or incorrect references to resources.

Issue 5: Performance and Scaling Issues

Slow stack operations, especially with large or complex templates.

Possible Causes

- Large templates with many resources can cause performance degradation.
- Resource contention or insufficient capacity in the OpenStack environment.
- Heat engine configuration not optimized for the scale of the operations.

Troubleshooting Steps

Break down large templates into smaller, modular templates that can be managed independently. Use nested stacks to handle complex deployments:

```
gitforgits_nested_stack:

  type: OS::Heat::Stack

  properties:

    template_url: <url_to_nested_template>
```

This approach allows for more manageable and efficient stack operations.

- If you are managing a large OpenStack environment, consider increasing the number of Heat engine workers to handle more concurrent operations. For this,
  - edit the **heat.conf** file:

```
sudo nano /etc/heat/heat.conf
```

    o   Increase the number of workers:

```
[DEFAULT]

num_engine_workers = <number_of_workers>
```

Use Ceilometer or other monitoring tools to track resource utilization and identify bottlenecks. Ensure that your OpenStack environment has sufficient capacity to handle the workload.

If the Heat engine itself is a bottleneck, consider deploying additional Heat engine instances to distribute the load. This can be done by deploying additional Heat services across multiple nodes in the OpenStack environment.

By understanding and addressing these challenges, such as stack creation failures, resource deletion issues, template validation errors, and performance bottlenecks, you can ensure that your orchestration tasks run smoothly and efficiently. With these troubleshooting strategies, you can effectively manage the cloud infrastructure, maintaining the benefits of Infrastructure as Code while you minimize the downtime and operational disruptions.

Summary

So, with this we have now completed our book and while learning this chapter, we had put Heat into use for orchestration and IaC operations. The chapter commenced with the installation and configuration of Heat bh, which facilitated the automated deployment and management of intricate cloud environments. Following this, the chapter investigated the development and deployment of Heat templates for stack management, which facilitated the automated generation of resources such as storage volumes, instances, and networks. In an effort to optimize performance and cost-efficiency, the utilization of auto-scaling with Heat and Ceilometer was implemented to dynamically adjust resources according to the workload.

Lastly, the chapter addressed common troubleshooting issues that may arise when utilizing Heat for orchestration tasks. These encompassed performance bottlenecks, resource deletion issues, stack creation and update failures, and template validation errors.

Index

Epilogue

On this, the last page of OpenStack Cookbook, I'd like to take a little time to thank you for joining me on this journey. A diverse array of problems has been addressed, encompassing the establishment of fundamental services such as Keystone and Nova, as well as the exploration of more complex subjects like auto-scaling using Heat and Ceilometer. These explorations were conducted against the backdrop of our fictitious company, GitforGits. The experiences of individuals have directly demonstrated the transformative potential of OpenStack in an organization's infrastructure, offering the necessary flexibility and control to thrive and adjust in the rapidly evolving digital environment of today.

The primary objective of this book was to explore dimensions of OpenStack beyond its technical components. The objective was to empower you with the assurance to tackle real-life challenges with pragmatic resolutions. Whether you are implementing new services, resolving problems, or enhancing your environment, the recipes we have discussed are specifically tailored to be immediately relevant to your operations. I trust that you have found them to be as beneficial and flexible as I deliberately intended. But beyond the particular tasks and challenges, I trust that this book has enabled you to see OpenStack not only as a tool, but also as a catalyst for innovation. Through the automation of deployments, efficient resource management, and the assurance of high availability, OpenStack enables you to concentrate on the core aspects of developing and delivering optimal services to your users and clients.

In this book, I've attempted to impart some of the wisdom I've gained from my personal encounters with OpenStack. Like everything else in the cloud computing world, OpenStack is always changing. In your ongoing engagement with OpenStack, I strongly urge you to persist in your exploration, experimentation, and relentless pursuit of the limits of what can be achieved. The skills acquired from this book will provide a solid basis, but the real potential of OpenStack does reside in its adaptability and the boundless opportunities it presents. I trust that OpenStack Cookbook will provide ongoing value as you proceed with the construction and administration of your cloud infrastructure. It is important to note that the solutions and recipes we have discussed are merely the initial stages. To fit your specific requirements, feel free to alter and build upon these as a foundation.

Thank you for dedicating your time to delve into these recipes with me. Having had the opportunity to impart my expertise and experience to you, I trust that you will depart from this book with a sense of empowerment to assume complete authority over your OpenStack environment. Based on my assessment, you now possess the necessary tools and knowledge to achieve success in areas such as performance optimization, operations scaling, and infrastructure security.

Wishing you ongoing success with OpenStack. Cultivate innovation, engage in exploration, and bear in mind—there is perpetually more to uncover.

Thank You

Made in the USA
Las Vegas, NV
14 January 2025

16406173R00160